GO DOWN, MOSES

NOTES

including
- *Life and Background*
- *McCaslin-Edmonds-Beauchamp History*
- *McCaslin Genealogy*
- *List of Characters*
- *Critical Commentaries*
    Was
    The Fire and the Hearth
    Pantaloon in Black
    The Old People
    The Bear, Parts 1, 2, 3, 4, 5
    Delta Autumn
    Go Down, Moses
- *Suggested Essay Questions*
- *Selected Bibliography*

by
James L. Roberts, Ph.D.
Professor of English
University of Nebraska

Cliffs Notes
INCORPORATED
LINCOLN, NEBRASKA 68501

Editor	Consulting Editor
Gary Carey, M.A.	*James L. Roberts, Ph.D.*
University of Colorado	*Department of English*
	University of Nebraska

Cliffs Notes, Inc.   Lincoln, Nebraska

CONTENTS

GO DOWN, MOSES
Notes

LIFE AND BACKGROUND

Even though William Faulkner is a contemporary American writer, he is already considered to be one of the world's greatest writers. In 1949, he was awarded the Nobel Prize for Literature, the highest literary prize that can be awarded to a writer. When he accepted this prize, he maintained that the duty of the artist was to depict the human heart in conflict with itself. In the book *Go Down, Moses*, this attitude is best realized in "The Bear," when Ike struggles to decide whether or not he can renounce his vast inheritance in order to atone for the sins of his lustful, miscegenetic forefather who amassed a fortune.

Faulkner was born in New Albany, Mississippi, on September 25, 1897, but his family soon moved to Oxford, Mississippi, and almost all of his novels take place in and around Oxford, which he renamed Jefferson in his stories and novels. Faulkner came from an old, proud, and distinguished Mississippi family, which included a governor, a colonel in the Confederate Army, and notable business pioneers. His great-grandfather, Colonel William Culbert Falkner (the "u" was added to Faulkner's name by mistake when his first novel was published, and Faulkner retained the misspelling), came to Mississippi from South Carolina during the first part of the nineteenth century.

The Colonel appears in many of Faulkner's novels under the name of Colonel John Sartoris. Colonel William Falkner had a rather distinguished career as a soldier both in the Mexican War and in the Civil War. During the Civil War, Falkner's hot temper caused him to be demoted from full Colonel to Lieutenant Colonel. After the war. Falkner was heavily involved in the trials of the Reconstruction period. He killed several men during this time and became a rather notorious figure. He also joined in with a partner and built the first railroad during Reconstruction. Then he quarreled with his partner, and the partnership broke up. When his former partner ran for the state legislature, Colonel Falkner ran against him and soundly defeated him.

Colonel Falkner also took out time to write one of the nation's best sellers, *The White Rose of Memphis,* which appeared in 1880. He also wrote two other novels, but only his first was an outstanding success. As was Colonel Sartoris in Faulkner's *The Unvanquished,* Colonel Falkner was finally killed by one of his rivals, and his death was never avenged. Today, one can travel to the cemetery in Holly Springs, Mississippi, and see a statue of Colonel Falkner, dressed in his Confederate uniform, gazing out at his railroad, and looking over the region that he fought so desperately and valiantly for. Only William Faulkner himself, of all the interceding members of the Falkner family, was as distinguished – and ultimately more distinguished – than his great-grandfather was.

Except for his novel *Sanctuary,* Faulkner's early novels were never commercial successes. Consequently, he would often interrupt a novel and write short stories for magazines. This is partially true of his novel *Go Down, Moses.* For example, "The Fire and the Hearth," one of the stories in the book, had appeared as a shorter story in *Collier's,* but it treated only the humorous conflict between Lucas Beauchamp and George Wilkins. The part of the story dealing with Lucas' outwitting the mine detector salesman with the salted buried treasure appeared as a separate story, entitled "Gold Is Not Always," in *The Atlantic Monthly.* When Faulkner arranged the novel later, he made certain changes in the two short stories and published them as one story.

Likewise, there are several versions of the short story "The Bear." A version of this story (without the long, complicated fourth section) appeared in *The Saturday Evening Post* on May 9, 1942. The fourth section appeared for the first time when the book *Go Down, Moses* was published. Likewise, "Pantaloon in Black," "The Old People" and the story "Go Down, Moses" appeared respectively in *Harper's Magazine,* October, 1940; *Harper's Magazine,* September, 1940; and *Collier's,* January 25, 1941.

Go Down, Moses marks the culmination in Faulkner's change from an early pessimistic attitude in his writing to a much more optimistic attitude. His technique of writing did not change, however. He still continued to present a protagonist in search of values in the modern world *through an evaluation of his responsibility to the past.*

Here, Isaac McCaslin examines the sin or guilt of his ancestors and decides to repudiate the land which he finds tainted. Ike is finally able to view the past honestly and then use his exploration of it for the formulation of positive values and constructive plans.

In Faulkner's new vision of optimism, he saw the world as capable of evolving decent and worthwhile values. Even in his stories presenting the white man attempting to keep the black man in bondage, or in his stories in which the white man fails to see the black man as an individual capable of love, hope, or salvation, Faulkner's tone is not one of despair and bitterness—rather, it is one of compassion toward the white man's *inability* to perceive his ignorance.

THE McCASLIN-EDMONDS-BEAUCHAMP HISTORY

Go Down, Moses, as we have said, was not published as a novel, with its material fresh and new. It was composed of several stories which had already been published separately, and there has always been a certain amount of confusion ever since the book was published about whether or not the book is a novel, and whether or not the individual stories can be significantly interrelated. Moreover, there is also the question of understanding the entire McCaslin thread that runs through the seemingly dissimilar stories that make up *Go Down, Moses*.

In a sense, it helps to review the McCaslin history, for even though some of the stories were originally published as separate entities, a full knowledge of the McCaslin family throws a different light on each individual story. For example, Uncle Buck's hunt for Tomey's Turl (a black man) in "Was" is somewhat modified by the fact that Tomey's Turl's father (a white man) is also Uncle Buck's father—*a fact that is not revealed in the short story*—and Uncle Buck's attempt to retrieve Tomey's Turl is based *not* on a desire to "capture" a runaway slave, but on Uncle Buck's attempt to avoid an encounter with the man-hunting Miss Sophonsiba.

The family heritage of the McCaslin family plays a major part in the entirety of *Go Down, Moses*, but we are not aware of the exact nature of that family heritage until Part 4 of "The Bear," which narrates the most crucial parts of the McCaslin history. Therefore, as we have said, it is useful to extract a general history of the family, as found in different sources and stories; it is reconstructed here in its most general outlines. It is important to note, however, that there are often discrepancies, or slight variations, or modifications, in some of the factual matters in the following history. Faulkner was, after all, an imaginative and creative writer—not a historian.

The patriarch-founder of the family, old Lucius Quintus Carothers McCaslin, was born in North Carolina, in 1772, and sometime during the late 1780s, he moved to northern Mississippi, and acquired, by some devious, dubious, and unknown means, a large tract of land from an Indian Chickasaw chief, Ikkemotubbe, who himself had acquired the land by underhanded, cruel, and manipulative methods.

Later, for Isaac (Ike), old McCaslin's grandson, the original purchase becomes suspect. That is, Chief Ikkemotubbe had no more right to *sell* the land than old McCaslin did to *buy* the land—for, according to Ike, "the land belong[s] to everyone as does the sky and the air." In addition, Ikkemotubbe also traded a quadroon (¾ white—¼ black) slave woman, her black husband, and her son by Ikkemotubbe (named Sam-Had-Two-Fathers, but shortened later to Sam Fathers) to old McCaslin for a gelding horse. Sam Fathers was, thus, born of a slave-mother, but his father was an Indian chief. He will become a permanent, key part of the McCaslin history. He will become Isaac's tutor and guide.

Then, by an unnamed wife, old McCaslin sired three children— the twins Theophilus (Uncle Buck) and Amodeus (Uncle Buddy) in about 1799, as well as an unnamed daughter who later married a man named Edmonds. Her descendants (the Edmondses) will be the final inheritors of the McCaslin lands and estates.

Around 1810, old McCaslin sired a child by his black slave Eunice. Then, twenty-two years later (1832), Eunice found out that her daughter by McCaslin, Tomasina (or Tomey), was pregnant by her father—old McCaslin himself. Unable to live with the terrible knowledge of the incest, Eunice committed suicide by drowning (on Christmas Day, 1832), an event which would later become a center of controversy in Uncle Buck's and Uncle Buddy's journal entries in Part 4 of "The Bear." Eunice's daughter, Tomasina, then gives birth to a three-fourths white son, who is named Terrel (but is called "Tomey's Turl"); he is raised as "special McCaslin property."

After old McCaslin's death, we learn, he provided a legacy of

$1,000.00 to be given to his son, Tomey's Turl, upon request. However, for some unexplained reason, Tomey's Turl never requested the legacy and, instead, contrived to live on the estate and to marry Tennie Beauchamp and sired six children by her – three of whom died in infancy. The three children who survived were James ("Tennie's Jim"), Fonsiba, and Lucas Beauchamp.

After Tomey's Turl never requested his legacy, Uncle Buck and Uncle Buddy increased the legacy: they stipulated that $1,000.00 was to be given to *each* of Tomey's Turl's children. Later, Ike tried unsuccessfully to deliver the legacy to Tennie's Jim, but he had disappeared up North. Ike followed Fonsiba to Arkansas, but he didn't leave the money with her; he deposited her share in an Arkansas bank, to be given to her in monthly allotments. The remaining son, Lucas, stayed on the plantation – specifically, on the 10 acres left by old McCaslin to Eunice's husband, Thucydus, who did not accept it.

When Lucas came of age, he demanded not only his own $1,000.00, but also the $1,000.00 that was left to his brother, Tennie's Jim, maintaining that he could look after the money as well as white folks could.

After old McCaslin's death, Uncle Buck and Uncle Buddy moved out of the unfinished plantation house and into a cabin that they had built themselves. They moved all of the Negro slaves into the unfinished plantation mansion. No windows had been installed, however, and yet despite that defect, the brothers made a ritual every night of locking the Negroes inside the house – even though later, they all climbed out the windows. And everyone, including Uncle Buck and Uncle Buddy, knew that this happened, but they pretended not to know because they relied on the blacks' sense of honor. And their trust was returned. All the blacks returned to the mansion before morning and were there waiting when Uncle Buck and Uncle Buddy came to unlock the doors.

Not believing in slavery, Uncle Buck and Uncle Buddy advocated a type of social philosophy that was radically different from the prevalent beliefs of the South. They believed that the "land did not belong to the people, but that people belonged to the land and that the earth would permit them to live on and out of it and use it only so long as they behaved, and that if they did not behave right, it [the land] would shake them off just like a dog getting rid of fleas" (from Faulkner's *The Unvanquished*).

These ideas, then, are the basis for Ike's eventual renunciation of his heritage. Even more radical, however, at least for those times, was Uncle Buck and Uncle Buddy's plans for the manumission of the slaves. That is, their slaves could earn their freedom by accumulated work. Unfortunately for the two twin uncles, the slaves, once freed, refused to leave, so that at the time of these early stories, there was an over-abundance of blacks on the McCaslin lands – thus accounting for Uncle Buck and Uncle Buddy's reluctance (in "Was") to purchase Tennie Beauchamp (yet another black slave) for Tomey's Turl to marry.

In 1850, McCaslin Edmonds ("Cass") is born to old McCaslin's grandson (a descendant of old McCaslin's daughter). Cass will inherit the McCaslin lands after Ike repudiates them. Cass is nine years old in the story "Was" and is often referred to as Ike's surrogate father because he is sixteen years older than Ike. He and Ike will examine the family journals in Part 4 of "The Bear."

During the Civil War, even though Uncle Buck and Uncle Buddy did not believe in slavery and had, in effect, "freed" all of their slaves, and even though their ideas were radically different from most Southerners, they were both fiercely loyal to the South, and they both wanted to enlist in Colonel Sartoris' Confederate regiment.

Because both men were about sixty-six, however, it was decided that only one of them could go fight in the Civil War. Consequently, a coin was tossed, allowing one of them to enlist in the Confederate Army. The loser would have to remain home and manage the plantation. Uncle Buck won the toss and went off to war. (In *The Unvanquished,* the decision is determined by a poker game between the twins. Uncle Buddy, the better poker player, wins the game and goes off to war.)

After the war ended, Uncle Buck, having successfully avoided being caught in matrimony by Miss Sophonsiba Beauchamp, married her, and they moved into the big plantation house, where Isaac Beauchamp McCaslin was born in 1867. This event, Isaac's birth, was commemorated by Ike's uncle (Hubert Beauchamp) ceremonially sealing up fifty gold pieces in a silver cup, to be presented to Ike on his twenty-first birthday. But by the time of Ike's twenty-first birthday, there was nothing but IOU's in a tin coffee pot, because Uncle Hubert needed the gold pieces – and the silver cup – to pay off gambling debts.

Ike was orphaned at a very early age; first, he lost his mother, and then, both his father ("Uncle Buck") and his uncle ("Uncle Buddy"); the twins died in the same year – just as they had both been born in the same year. Consequently, Ike was reared partly by his sixteen-year-old cousin Cass (McCaslin Edmonds).

When Ike was still very young, Sam Fathers (the son of the old Chickasaw chief Ikkemotubbe) began tutoring him in the art, craft, mysteries, and rituals of hunting so that by the time Ike was eight years old, he had mastered all of the basics of the hunt ("The Old People": "He had learned when to shoot, and when not to shoot, when to kill and when not to kill,and better, what to do with it afterward.").

When Ike was ten years old, Sam realized that he had taught Ike everything he could teach him about the world of "civilization," so he moved into a cabin in the wilderness. But for the next six years, he continued to teach Ike more about hunting. Now, however, he taught him how to hunt for the big game – the deer and the bears. Under Sam's tutelage, Ike killed his first deer, and he was ceremoniously baptised with the deer's fresh blood. Afterward, Ike was recognized as being ready to be a participant in the great annual pageant, the ritual hunt – the hunt for Old Ben, the giant bear which is finally killed during Ike's sixteenth year.

That same year, Ike discovered the old ledgers that his father and Uncle Buddy had kept during the years past. By pondering over them, Ike was finally able to come to the horrible realization that his grandfather, old McCaslin, seduced (or "ordered to bed") a slave named Eunice, who bore him a daughter named Tomasina (called "Tommy" or "Tomey"). Then, twenty-two years later, old McCaslin *committed incest with his own mulatto daughter,* who bore him a male child, named Terrel (called "Tomey's Turl").

Adopting and expanding the views of his father and Uncle Buddy about the ownership of land and the curse of slavery, and feeling that the land was further cursed by old McCaslin's, his grandfather's, inhuman acts, Ike, at age twenty-one, *renounces his inheritance* – declaring that God meant for *all the land to be free,* like the air we breathe.

The entire property, then, went to Ike's cousin McCaslin (Cass) Edmonds (a descendant of old McCaslin through McCaslin's daughter) and Cass' descendants.

Then Ike, in emulation of the Ancient Nazarene (Christ), became a carpenter, and he later married a young girl who had dreams of becoming the mistress of the great McCaslin mansion and plantation.

McCASLIN GENEALOGY

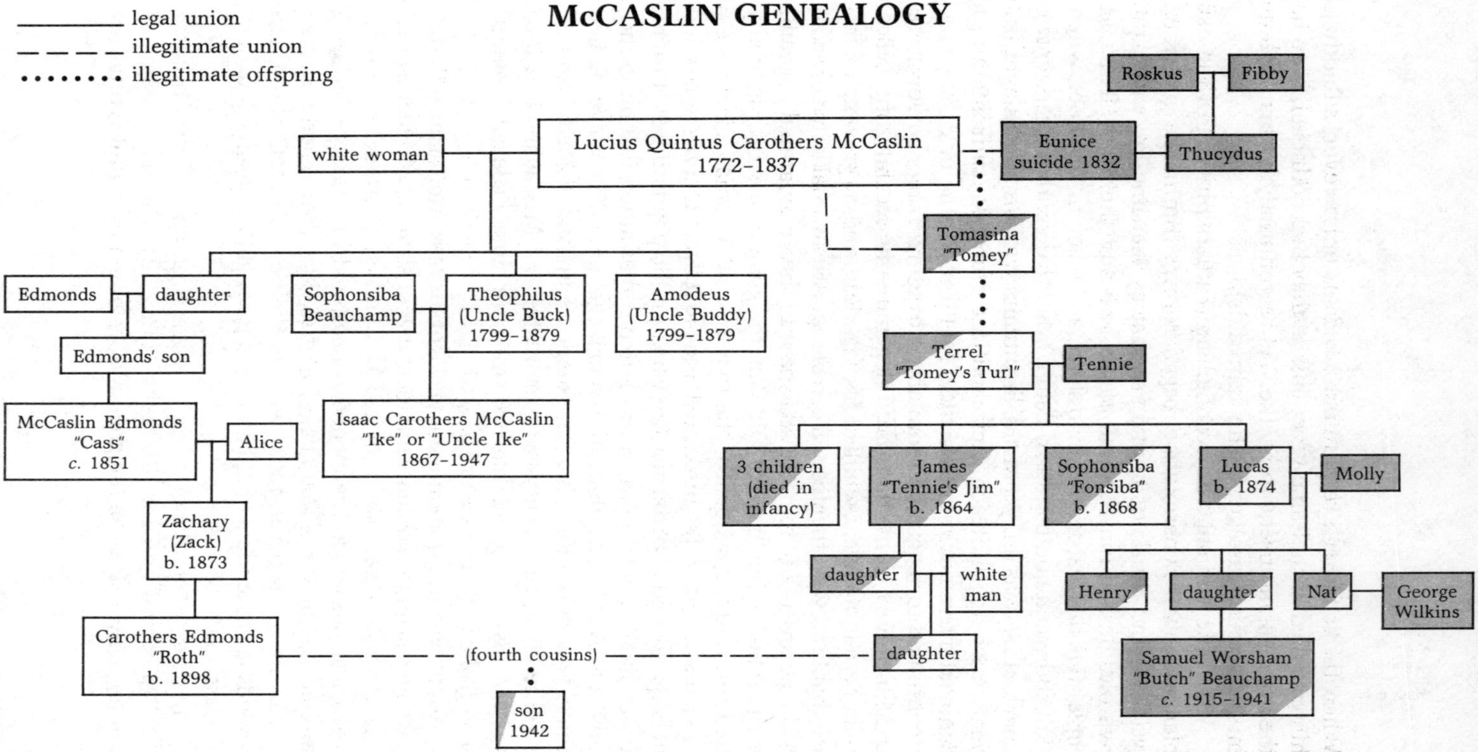

When Ike refused to reclaim his inheritance, however, she refused him her bed. Thus Ike, forever childless, became "Uncle Ike" to half the county – and father to no one. Yet he continued his annual hunts in the wilderness, even as he approached eighty.

During this time, Cass' son Zachary (Zack) inherited the McCaslin plantation, and when Zack's son, Carothers (Roth), was born, and when Zack's wife died in childbirth, Lucas Beauchamp's wife, Molly (who was the midwife), had to nurse both her black son, Henry, and the white child, Roth Edmonds.

After Molly had lived in Zack's house for six months, however, Lucas, remembering old McCaslin's affairs with his black slaves, suddenly became jealous of Zack, and in a dramatic confrontation, he demanded the return of his wife, Molly.

Molly returned, but as sometimes happened among young white and black children at that time, Henry (the black child of the Beauchamps) and Roth (the white child of the Edmondses) grew up together almost as brothers – until, at a certain age, the eternal curse of racism descended upon them. Then they were forever separated, the white man from the black man.

When Roth was grown, he took his old kinsman Uncle Ike on the annual great hunt in the wilderness. There, Uncle Ike was confronted by a woman whom Roth had previously had an affair with and whose infant son she now carried in her arms. Upon investigation, it was revealed that the woman had a small amount of black blood and was the great-great-granddaughter of old McCaslin. (By Southern standards, she was "black" simply because she had a tiny trace of black blood and despite the fact that she passed for white.) Moreover, to Ike's horror, she had had sex with Roth, who was her kinsman, the great-great-great-grandson of old McCaslin.

Once again, the black and white descendants of old McCaslin are united. And once again, both woman and child are rejected by the white side of the family for one reason only: because of the miniscule amount of black blood that both the woman and the child carry.

LIST OF CHARACTERS

Beauchamp, Henry ("The Fire and the Hearth")

Lucas and Molly's son (black), who grew up as a brother to Roth

Edmonds (white) until one day when the gulf of the races, "the haughty ancestral pride," separated them briefly, and then, out of shame, forever.

Beauchamp, James (Tennie's Jim) Thucydus
("The Fire and the Hearth," "The Bear")

The oldest son of Tomey's Turl and Tennie Beauchamp, who, as a youth, worked at the hunting camps mainly overseeing the dogs. In "The Bear," when he could have collected his $1,000.00 legacy, he disappeared on his twenty-first birthday. In "The Fire and the Hearth," he ran away before he came of age. Later, Ike tries unsuccessfully to trace him down to deliver his legacy. The legacy will later be claimed by his younger brother, Lucas Beauchamp.

Beauchamp, Hubert (Fitz-Hubert) ("Was," "The Bear")

The owner of a large plantation (called "Warwick" by Hubert's sister, Sophonsiba) located in a neighboring county of Yoknapatawpha. He is a bachelor who wants to get his sister, Miss Sophonsiba, married off so that he can live a peaceful life. He is also the owner of the slave Tennie, whom the McCaslin twins are forced to buy so as to preserve Uncle Buck's bachelorhood. Ultimately, however, Mr. Hubert *does* become Uncle Buck's brother-in-law, as well as Isaac's uncle and godfather. In "The Bear," we hear how Hubert sealed away fifty pieces of gold for Ike in a *silver* cup. But when Ike opened the gift on his twenty-first birthday, there was only a pile of IOU's in a *tin* coffee pot.

Beauchamp, Lucas ("The Fire and the Hearth,"
"The Bear," Part 4)

Lucas is the youngest son of Tomey's Turl and Tennie, and thus, he is the grandson of old L. Q. C. McCaslin. He is the only descendant to remain on the McCaslin plantation, living on the ten acres that was originally left for Thucydus, Eunice's husband, who did not accept it, and so it passed on to Tomey's Turl, who ignored it. Ultimately, it came into Lucas' possession, along with the inheritance money from old McCaslin. Clearly, Lucas is the arrogant and proud type who will claim everything that is his. Early in his marriage, his wife, Molly, is staying with the white "master," Zack Edmonds, in order to nurse Zack's child. After six months, though, Lucas becomes jealous (probably without cause), and although he's black, he challenges the white man—and wins. Later, he becomes involved with making bootleg whiskey on the McCaslin farm; he is caught and becomes involved with the courts. He also involves himself with a "divining machine" in order to find buried treasure; in fact, he becomes so involved in searching for gold that he almost loses his wife through divorce. He finally comes to his senses and returns to the fire and the hearth.

Beauchamp, Molly ("The Fire and the Hearth"),
Mollie ("Go Down, Moses")

Lucas' wife, who represents the eternal mother figure. When Zack Edmonds' wife dies in childbirth, Molly moves into his house, along with her newborn black child, Henry, and nurses both babies. Later, threatening divorce, she forces Lucas to give up his "immoral" pursuit of buried treasure.

In "Go Down, Moses," as Aunt Mollie, she senses that something is wrong with her lost grandson, so she asks the local lawyer, Gavin Stevens, to find him. When she discovers that he is dead, it does not matter to her that he was executed as the convicted murderer of a policeman in Chicago. She simply wants his body returned home for burial, along with all the proper rites due to a dead grandson.

Beauchamp, Samuel Worsham (Butch) ("Go Down, Moses")

Mollie Beauchamp's grandson, whom she raised and who was thrown off the McCaslin plantation by Roth for stealing from the plantation commissary. After Butch is executed, Mollie wants his body returned to her with all the proper rites.

Beauchamp, Sophonsiba Miss ("Was," "The Bear," Part 4)

Mr. Hubert's "man-hunting" single sister, who is hunting a husband in "Was." She "sets a trap" for Uncle Buck, which he falls into, only to be rescued by Uncle Buddy. She will, however, later marry Uncle Buck, live in the McCaslin mansion, and will become the mother of Isaac McCaslin.

Beauchamp, Sophonsiba (Fonsiba) ("The Bear," Part 4)

Fonsiba is the daughter of Tomey's Turl and Tennie Beauchamp and is about ⅜ white. At eighteen, she marries an impractical idealist who believes that the Civil War has set the Negroes free and, therefore, he doesn't have to work any more. When she is twenty-one, Isaac tracks her down in order to give her the $1,000.00 legacy, but seeing the desolate condition of her Arkansas farm and the irresponsibility of her husband, he deposits the money in a bank and arranges for her to get $3.00 a month so that she won't starve.

Beauchamp, Tennie ("Was," "The Fire and the Hearth," "The Bear," Part 4)

A slave girl belonging to Hubert Beauchamp who is the object of Tomey's Turl's love. She is seen only in the fourth section of "Was," in the McCaslin wagon, thus revealing to us that she has been won by Uncle Buddy in the poker game and that she will be able to marry Tomey's Turl (the black son of old McCaslin). They and their descendants will henceforth use the name Beauchamp—not McCaslin—as their last name.

Birdsong ("Pantaloon in Black")

The white night watchman who runs a crooked dice game. When Rider catches him cheating, Birdsong draws a pistol, and Rider kills him with a razor. Birdsong's relatives then lynch Rider.

Brownlee, Percival, later renamed Spintrius ("The Bear," Part 4)

A slave bought from Bedford Forrest. The reason for the purchase is never revealed, and the purchase seems strange because at the time of the purchase, Uncle Buck and Uncle Buddy were ridding themselves of all slaves. Conjecturally, Brownlee was bought to keep books, a job which he couldn't do; in fact, Brownlee couldn't do anything. The brothers tried to free him, but he wouldn't leave. In later years, Brownlee emerges as the proprietor of a well-established New Orleans house of prostitution.

Compson, General ("The Old People," "The Bear")

One of the respected men of Jefferson and one of the expert and "true" hunters.

Crawford, Doc ("The Bear," Part 4)

After the last encounter with Old Ben, when Lion and Boon Hogganbeck are wounded and Sam Fathers collapses, the wounded Boon fetches Doc Crawford to administer, first, to Lion, replacing his innards and sewing him up, and then to Sam Fathers, who "just quit." Finally, after the massive dog and the old wilderness guide are cared for, Boon allows himself to be treated.

De Spain, Major ("The Old People," "The Bear")

The owner of the large tracts of land which constitute the part of the wilderness where the men hunt. After the deaths of Old Ben (the great bear) and Sam Fathers, de Spain sells large portions of this land to the lumber companies.

De Vitry, Chevalier Soeur-Blonde ("The Old People")

The Frenchman from New Orleans who gives Ikkemotubbe the name of "Du Homme," which is corrupted into "doom."

Edmonds, McCaslin (Cass) ("Was," "The Fire and the Hearth," "The Old People," "The Bear")

Cass is the great-grandson of L. Q. C. McCaslin through his grandmother, who was old McCaslin's daughter. Cass is the person who participated in the events of "Was" and subsequently told them to Ike. Also, at the end of "The Old People," he reveals that he underwent the same mystical experience that Ike just underwent in the wilderness. In "The Bear," he enters into the long, involved conversation with Ike concerning the nature of inheritance and the ownership of land. When Ike finally renounces his inheritance, Cass becomes the owner of the McCaslin estate, providing Ike with enough to sustain him.

18

Edmonds, Carothers (Roth) ("The Fire and the Hearth," "Delta Autumn")

The great-great-great-grandson of old McCaslin and, therefore, he is the first cousin, twice removed, of Isaac McCaslin. He is the owner and present manager of the McCaslin estates. In "The Fire and the Hearth," Roth was originally nursed by Molly, and he still holds her in high regard. When she comes to him, wanting a divorce from Lucas, he is deeply concerned for her. Later, he is infuriated when he learns that bootleg whiskey has been made on his plantation.

In "Delta Autumn," we find out that Roth had an affair with an unnamed woman (with some black blood); they lived in New Mexico the preceding winter for six weeks, a place where they could live as man and wife without arousing suspicion. On the way to the annual hunt, Roth sees this woman standing by the road with her newborn baby, Roth's child. She had previously agreed not to see Roth anymore, and he had sent money for the birth of the child. Now, however, she wants to see him again. Before she arrives, Roth leaves money with Uncle Ike, with the simple message of "No" to tell her. Ike discovers that the woman is the great-great-granddaughter of old McCaslin, descending through the Negro side—and he is horrified.

Edmonds, Zack ("The Fire and the Hearth")

Roth's father. When his wife died in childbirth, he asked Molly to nurse both her child and his own. Later, when Molly's husband, Lucas, became jealous, Roth had to face Lucas in a physical showdown which Zack lost, but with dignity.

Eunice ("The Bear," Part 4)

A slave owned by old McCaslin. When it is discovered that she is pregnant by old McCaslin, she is married off to Thucydus. When later she discovers that their daughter, Tomasina, is also pregnant by old McCaslin, Eunice cannot face the shame of the incest, and so she drowns herself, on Christmas Day, 1832.

Ewell, Walter ("The Old People," "The Bear")

One of the "true hunters," whose rifle "never missed."

Fathers, Sam ("The Old People," "The Bear," "Delta Autumn")

Sam is Ike's hunting teacher and, ultimately, he is Ike's spiritual guide. He first teaches Ike all he knows about basic hunting; he is behind the boy, guiding him when he kills his first rabbit at eight. As the boy grew, Sam became the guide who introduced Ike into the virtues of a manhood lived in close communion with nature and, ultimately, he led him into the mysteries of the wilderness and of life itself.

Sam Fathers' name comes from the fact that his real father was the Indian chief Ikkemotubbe, who arranged for Sam's mother, a quadroon slave woman, to be married to a black slave; his original name, "Sam-Had-Two-Fathers," became shortened to simply "Sam Fathers."

Sam is a product of many bloods, all of which influence his many actions. Technically, Sam is ½ Indian, ⅜ white, and ⅛ Negro, but in the South at that time, he was, racially speaking, a Negro – even though he never lived as a black man, nor was he ever treated as one. Sam's pride, knowledge, and heritage, derived from Indian chiefs, determine his unique life-style.

Sam's various bloods give him qualities of all of them, but, ultimately, in his life in the wilderness and in his association with others, and finally, in his death wish, it is always the Indian blood which seems dominant. When Sam introduces Ike to the Great Buck, the spirit of the wilderness, Sam addresses the buck in the language of his Indian forbears. As Ike's spiritual guide, Sam is associated with all of the noble Indian qualities related with a pure and innocent life lived in close communion with nature.

After Sam has invested Ike with all of his knowledge of the wilderness, and after he has seen the death of Old Ben, the great bear and the symbol of the wilderness, Sam is ready for death. He instructs Boon and Ike to arrange his burial in the customary Indian fashion – by ceremonial cremation. After Sam's death, Ike returns one more time to visit Sam's grave. He is able to feel Sam's presence still roaming through what is left of the "ruined wilderness."

Hogganbeck, Boon ("The Old People," "The Bear")

Boon is part Indian; his grandmother was a Chickasaw. He is very tall, very ugly, and he possesses the mind of a child. He feels very close to Sam Fathers, and he is fiercely loyal to Major de Spain, to

Cass, and to Isaac McCaslin. He is a notoriously bad shot, unable to hit anything, yet he is devoted to hunting and to the wilderness. After Sam Fathers tames the fierce Lion, Boon develops a deep love for the savage dog. At the end of Part 3 of "The Bear," when Lion is wounded and Sam Fathers collapses, Boon demonstrates extraordinary strength and fortitude in caring for both man and dog, even though he himself is seriously wounded and in need of medical attention. At the end of "The Bear," it seems as though his simple mind cannot comprehend the forthcoming destruction of the wilderness.

Ikkemotubbe (Doom) ("The Old People," "The Bear," "Delta Autumn")

The Indian chief from whom L. Q. C. McCaslin purchased his original tract of land. Earlier, Ikkemotubbe had left the Indian land and traveled to New Orleans, where he acquired the French name of "Du Homme" (the Man), which became shortened to "Doom," a particularly apt name since Ikkemotubbe contributed to the doom of certain old values. Returning from New Orleans, he gave demonstrations using a white powder and, suddenly, there were the mysterious deaths of two puppies *and* Moketubbe's year-old son. As a result, Moketubbe resigned, and Ikkemotubbe became the new chief.

Issetibbeha ("The Old People")

The old Indian chief of the Chickasaws, he was a proud and noble chief, and in "The Old People," it is he whom Sam Fathers addresses when he says, "Oleh, Grandfather."

Jobaker ("The Old People")

A Chickasaw Indian whose only friend is Sam Fathers. Jobaker lives in the Bottom, and when he dies, Sam Fathers buries him in a secret place and then burns down his shack.

Ketcham ("Pantaloon in Black")

The jailor who locks Rider up after the Birdsong slaying.

Legate, Will ("Delta Autumn")

He is the son of one of the original "true hunters" in the wilderness;

he is also a hunter, and apparently, he knows about Roth's affair with the unnamed woman. He is constantly punning on Roth's interest in "does," an obvious allusion to Roth's affair with the woman whom they saw standing by the road.

McCaslin, Amodeus (Uncle Buddy) ("Was," "The Bear")

One of the twin sons of L. Q. C. McCaslin, who, along with his twin, Uncle Buck, moves out of the McCaslin mansion after the death of their father and begins the systematic method of allowing the slaves to earn their freedom (manumission). Uncle Buddy is the better poker player of the two, and he is called upon at the end of "Was" to use his ability to retrieve his brother from the clutches of matrimony, a situation that hung on the outcome of a critical poker game.

McCaslin, Isaac (Ike or Uncle Ike) ("Was," "The Old People," "The Bear," "Delta Autumn")

Isaac is the son of Theophilus (Uncle Buck) McCaslin and Sophonsiba Beauchamp, and he is the grandson of old L. Q. C. McCaslin. Not only is he the central figure in "The Bear," "The Old People," and "Delta Autumn," but he also appears, or is mentioned, in numerous other works by Faulkner. (In *Intruder in the Dust,* 1948, Ike is still alive at age ninety.)

In "The Old People," Ike is a young boy in the process of learning about hunting – how to shoot, when to shoot, and what to do with the game after it has been killed. At first, Ike must be initiated into the simplest aspects of hunting, as when Sam Fathers teaches him how to load his first gun and to kill his first running rabbit, when Ike is only eight years old. Later, when Ike is ten, he has learned everything about hunting that can be learned on the plantation; now he is ready, according to Sam Fathers, for the big game in the wilderness.

In the wilderness, Ike's education continued under the tutelage of Sam Fathers. First, he had to learn that the wilderness was *not* dangerous. Since he was the youngest of the hunters, he was, of course, allotted the poorest stands. Accordingly, Ike learned patience and humility, and under Sam's tutelage, he learned all of the proper rites of the hunting, so that when he killed his first deer, Sam Fathers took some of the deer's blood and baptised him into the rituals of

22

hunting and manhood. "Sam Fathers marked his face with the hot blood which he had spilled, and he ceased to be a child and became a hunter and a man." This statement will become the metaphor for Ike's initiation into the mysteries of the wilderness, and this event will often be recalled, even in "Delta Autumn," when Ike is in his seventies.

After the initiation into the wilderness and into manhood, Ike is now ready to be initiated into the great mysteries of the wilderness, as represented by the Great Buck, whom Sam addressed as "Oleh, Chief . . . Grandfather." With this scene, Ike is forever invested with the spirit of the wilderness, and he inherits from Sam all of the noble and mystical qualities gained from a close communion with the wilderness.

In "The Bear," at age sixteen, Ike knows the wilderness better than any man; he knows trails that even Sam Fathers does not know. He is now so respected by the other hunters that they expect Ike to assume the ritualistic duty of killing Old Ben, the bear who is a symbol of the pure spirit of the wilderness. Earlier, in order to merely *see* Old Ben, Ike had to shed all of his instruments of civilization—his gun and his compass—and he was awarded a close view of the magnificent bear.

After the death of the bear, Ike is saddened by the destruction of the wilderness and the intrusion of civilization upon this virgin territory. But, using the values that he learned from the wilderness, and the purity of life which symbolized the freedom of the wilderness, Ike was able to evaluate his relationship to his inheritance and to realize that God did not intend for man to own land—that land was meant to be as free as the air we breathe; if man parcels out portions of land, this is a violation of the trust which God put in man. Therefore, man will bring a curse upon himself.

When Ike discovers the sexual sins of his old ancestor, Lucius Quintus Carothers McCaslin, he utilizes the values which he discovered from a life lived in simplicity and purity, in close communion with the wilderness; in this way, he is able to repudiate and renounce his inheritance and his patrimony and to assume the life of a simple carpenter, in emulation of the life lived by the Ancient Nazarene.

Ike, however, does marry, but when his wife cannot force him (by tempting him with her naked body) to assume proprietorship of both the McCaslin plantation and the great McCaslin mansion, she denies Ike her body. Thus, Ike is left forever without progeny, and he becomes "Uncle Ike" to half the county, but father to no one.

In "Delta Autumn," Ike is in his seventies and has the unpleasant task of paying off Roth's mistress and dismissing her. But when he discovers that the mistress is part black *and* white and that she is a direct descendant of Ike's white grandfather, old McCaslin, Ike is horrified beyond measure at the prospect of a union between Roth and the woman, his fourth cousin.

McCaslin, Lucius Quintus Carothers (in passing)

He is the progenitor of three principal families – the white McCaslins, the female (distaff side) line of the Edmondses, and the racially mixed line of the Beauchamps. He arrived in Mississippi from Carolina and purchased a large tract of land from the Chickasaw chief Ikkemotubbe and established his estate. He is the father of three white children: Uncle Buck (Theophilus or "Filus"), Uncle Buddy (Amodeus), and an unnamed daughter who marries an Edmonds. Through his black slave Eunice, and then through his own daughter by Eunice, Tomasina, McCaslin sires the black side of the family, which takes the last name of Beauchamp (pronounced "Beecham").

McCaslin, Theophilus (Uncle Buck or "Filus")
("Was," "The Bear")

One of the twin sons of L. Q. C. McCaslin; he joins his brother in moving out of the mansion after the death of their father and begins their plans for the manumission of all of the slaves, who, once freed, refuse to leave. In "Was," Uncle Buck goes out to retrieve the runaway Tomey's Turl, and he finds himself "trapped" by Miss Sophonsiba Beauchamp. Even though he escapes matrimony (at that time), he later marries her, and in his old age, he becomes the father of Isaac.

Mannie ("Pantaloon in Black")

Rider's wife of six months whom he desperately loved. Her spirit seems to appear to him shortly after her death, and his only wish is to join her.

Maydew ("Pantaloon in Black")

The sheriff who arrests Rider.

Moketubbe ("The Old People")

Issetibbeha's weak, fat, and lazy son who succeeds his father, but when his cousin Ikkemotubbe returns and demonstrates his power by using strange drugs and powders, Moketubbe, fearing for his life, abdicates in favor of his cousin, Ikkemotubbe.

Phoebe (Fibby) ("The Bear," Part 4)

See **Roscius**

Rider ("Pantaloon in Black")

The Negro sawmill worker whose wife of six months has just died. In his desperate grief, Rider furiously helps bury her, then returns to work (while all the white folks think he would undoubtedly "use the excuse" of his wife's death to take a day off); he performs superhuman tasks, gets drunk, and enters into a crooked dice game with a white man named Birdsong. When the white man is caught cheating and draws a pistol, Rider slashes his throat. Later, Birdsong's relatives hang Rider from the bell rope in the Negro school house.

Roscius (Roskus) and Phoebe (Fibby) ("The Bear," Part 4)

Slaves owned by old McCaslin. At his death in 1837, they were freed, but did not want to leave. They are the parents of Thucydus.

Sheriff's Deputy ("Pantaloon in Black")

This man is never named, but in the last part of the story, he describes to his wife all of the events which Rider participates in after the death of his wife. The deputy cannot understand anyone acting the way Rider did, since he cannot understand that a Negro is capable of true, deep love and grief. Without being named, the deputy represents the blindness of the white man concerning the depth of true feelings within a black man.

Stevens, Gavin ("Go Down, Moses")

The attorney with a Phi Beta Kappa key from Harvard and a Ph.D. in law from Heidelberg; he is retranslating the New Testament from Greek into Hebrew. He is responsible for arranging for Samuel Worsham Beauchamp's body to be returned to Jefferson; he is collecting money from the townspeople and paying for the rest himself.

Tennie

See **Beauchamp, Tennie**

Thucydus ("The Bear," Part 4)

Fibby and Roskus' son. When Eunice became pregnant (by old McCaslin), old MacCaslin apparently "arranged" for Eunice to marry Thucydus, to whom he left ten acres of prime farm land, land which will remain in the Beauchamp family, and on which Lucas Beauchamp lives.

Tomasina (Tomy, or Tomey) ("The Bear")

The mulatto daughter of old McCaslin and Eunice, a slave woman. After an incestuous relationship with her father, old McCaslin, Tomasina gives birth to Terrel, better known as Tomey's Turl.

Tomey's Turl (Tomasina's Terrel) ("Was," "The Fire and the Hearth," "The Bear," Part 4)

One of the McCaslins' so-called slaves. He is a three-fourths (quadroon) brother to Uncle Buck and Uncle Buddy, even though this fact is never mentioned. His love for Mr. Hubert Beauchamp's slave girl, Tennie, and his later marriage to Tennie will establish the last name of *Beauchamp* for all of their descendants, which will include Tennie's Jim, Fonsiba, and Lucas Beauchamp.

Uncle Ash ("The Old People," "The Bear")

The old Negro cook who has done the cooking for the camp for so long that he pays no attention to the time of the day, often serving breakfast at 2 a.m. and the mid-day meal at 9 a.m. In "The Bear," he sulks one day until all of the hunters agree to let him try to kill a bear with some shells that were given to him long ago. After the attempt, he is content to return to cooking.

Wilkins, George ("The Fire and the Hearth")

Lucas' inept son-in-law. Knowing that George is making bootleg whiskey, Lucas is anxious for him to be caught, not because of the competition, but because George is so inept that he will ruin all the chances for everyone to profit. Later, however, Lucas is forced to accept George as a partner in the bootlegging enterprise.

Wilkins, Nathalie Beauchamp ("The Fire and the Hearth")

Lucas' daughter, who is secretly married to George Wilkins. But she will not move into George's cabin until Lucas has paid for a new porch and a well so that she won't have to carry water.

Wilmoth ("Go Down, Moses")

The newspaper editor in "Go Down, Moses" who helps Gavin Stevens bring back the body of Samuel Worsham Beauchamp. At first, he agrees to Stevens' request not to print the news that Samuel was executed as a murderer so as to protect Mollie Beauchamp; he is therefore surprised later when Mollie wants everything about her grandson printed in the paper.

Worsham, Hamp ("Go Down, Moses")

Mollie Beauchamp's brother. Both he and his sister were children of a slave owned by Miss Belle Worsham; he has remained in her service all his life.

Worsham, Miss Belle ("Go Down, Moses")

The elderly spinster who was raised almost like a sister with the black Mollie Beauchamp, whose brother still works for Miss Worsham. She feels very sympathetic to Mollie's grief, which she calls "our grief." And even though she cannot afford it, she takes money from her meager savings to help arrange for Samuel Worsham Beauchamp's body to be returned to town for proper burial.

WAS

The first story in this novel is one of Faulkner's finest works of humor, even though some readers have complained that the complexity of the story (especially the language) prevents them from grasping the humor. Besides the sometimes troublesome language in "Was," the point-of-view of the story is also very different, and sometimes difficult. The story is told as though the events occurred in a time that *was* instead of in a time that *is*; that is, Isaac ("Ike") McCaslin, the central figure of the novel, does *not* narrate this story but, instead, *Faulkner reports a story which Ike heard* from his cousin Cass many times. We read that "this was not something participated in [by Ike] . . . but by his elder cousin, McCaslin Edmonds." The story, then, a long-familiar story to Ike, begins with a concern about ancestry and heredity, a theme which becomes one of the book's central concerns.

"Was" is basically related to the other stories in that it presents the idyllic life that Theophilus (Uncle Buck) McCaslin and his twin brother, Amodeus (Uncle Buddy) McCaslin, lead as bachelors just prior to the Civil War, and it also introduces us to Isaac's mother-to-be in the role of the man-hunting aristocrat of the woods, Miss Sophonsiba Beauchamp (pronounced in Mississippi as "Beacham," or more dialectically as "Beechum").

Part 1 of "Was" is important primarily because it presents the main character of this novel: Isaac ("Ike") McCaslin, even though Ike is not born at the time of "Was" (1859). In particular, this first section describes and illustrates the ideas and moral concerns of Ike's people, beliefs which they held and lived by some seven or eight years before Ike's birth. Later, we will see that Ike himself holds these same moral concerns. Yet none of this is stated directly by Faulkner; we must listen to all of the small details that are an important, though not an obvious, part of his storyteller's voice, and we must realize how very much like a real teller of stories Faulkner's narrative voice is.

For example, note the first sentence. It is not a sentence at all. It is simply a loose statement, containing no subject nor verb and no end punctuation, but it holds key information about Ike. We will not discover this information fully illustrated until the next-to-the-last story, "Delta Autumn," but already, Faulkner injects it into our subconscious, as it were, as we read his irregular, river-like narrative. His technique becomes even richer upon a second reading, but by knowing *beforehand* what is packed into these early fragment-like statements, we can realize a fuller dimension to the novel, and we can discover the quintessence of its central character, Ike McCaslin.

In summary, Part 1 of "Was" is a loosely told "hunt story," but it is far more than merely a humorous tale about an adventure that happened in backwoods country years ago. It contains the pervading moral beliefs and concepts of Ike McCaslin — concepts and beliefs that he has inherited from his forefathers and which he lives by.

Concerning this matter of Ike's inheriting moral beliefs, note that Faulkner, in passing, focuses on what Ike inherits materially — that is, land and property. Faulkner says that Ike does not believe in owning land: "[He] owned no property and never desired to since the earth was no man's but all men's . . ."

This basic idea is introduced early because of Ike's later rejection of his inheritance in the center of the novel (Part 4 of "The Bear"). Likewise, Ike's decision not to own land is directly related to Uncle Buddy and Uncle Buck's advanced social ideas about manumission; that is, they do not believe in owning slaves, and they are letting their slaves earn their freedom by working it out in wages. This fact is not mentioned in "Was," but it helps our understanding of this particular story if we know about it, for we can then better understand *why* Uncle Buck and Uncle Buddy were *so reluctant* to buy another slave (Tennie); obviously, they have more slaves now than they know what to do with, because most of the slaves who have earned their freedom do not leave the home place. They stay on.

Part 1 of the story also describes Ike's love of the wilderness — a wilderness which, during the course of Ike's life, will be greatly diminished. About Ike's love of the wilderness, or the woods, Faulkner says, ". . . he [Ike] loved the woods: [he] owned no property . . . since the earth was no man's but all men's, as light and air and weather were." Thus, this first, brief section of the story has little or nothing to do with the main narrative of "Was"; rather, it is a sort of introduction to the entire novel and an introduction to Ike as the main character of the novel, and it also presents background information about him, as well as about the more important concerns of the work.

In Part 2 of "Was," Faulkner recreates the type of society which existed before Ike was born, and more important, he depicts the type of person Ike's father-to-be (Uncle Buck) is and how Ike's future mother (Miss Sophonsiba) pursues Uncle Buck. Likewise, we meet young McCaslin Edmonds (Cass), who will figure prominently in the intense discussion of heredity and morality in Part 4 of "The Bear."

"Was" is a masterfully constructed work whose humor is based on the interplay between three levels of "hunting." For example, Part 2 opens with a hilarious account of the "fox hunt" which takes place inside Uncle Buck and Uncle Buddy's cabin: the fox is chased from the kitchen to the hall to the dogs' room to the bedrooms to the kitchen again, and finally it is "treed" behind the clock on the mantle.

At the end of the "fox hunt," Uncle Buck arrives during all the confusion, and he adds more excitement by declaring that "Tomey's Turl has broke out again." We then discover that Tomey's Turl slips off twice a year to visit Tennie, a female slave who is owned by Mr. Hubert Beauchamp and his unmarried sister, Miss Sophonsiba, who live at (what Miss Sophonsiba calls) Warwick Plantation. Mr. Hubert will *not* buy Tomey's Turl because he is "a damned half-white McCaslin," and Uncle Buck and Uncle Buddy will *not* buy Tennie for Tomey's Turl because they have too many slaves already, all of whom they are in the process of setting free.

Uncle Buck eats a fast breakfast, puts on a tie, then takes young Cass with him, and together, they begin the "hunt" for Tomey's Turl. Uncle Buddy warns Cass to come back and get him, Uncle Buddy, if anything "begins to look wrong."

About three miles from Mr. Hubert's, Uncle Buck and Cass spot Tomey's Turl astride a slow mule about a mile ahead of them, and Uncle Buck decides to take off as fast as his horse, Black John, can race ahead and cut him off, but Tomey's Turl is aware of the situation and is able to elude Uncle Buck.

Cass and Uncle Buck arrive at Mr. Hubert's at noon, just in time for "dinner" (as the noon meal is called), presided over by Miss Sophonsiba Beauchamp. While the two men, Uncle Buck and Mr. Hubert, take an afternoon nap (after Uncle Buck drinks two toddies that "Sibbey" [Miss Sophonsiba] brings him), Cass comes upon Tomey's Turl in the back yard, and he discovers that the "half-white" has "secret help" in his romantic adventures (apparently, Miss Sophonsiba is help-

ing the two lovers – Tomey's Turl and Tennie – elude Uncle Buck so
that she can keep Uncle Buck at Warwick for a longer time). Inter-
estingly, Tomey's Turl does not seem too concerned about the possibility or the consequences of Uncle Buck's catching him.

After their naps, Uncle Buck and Mr. Hubert and Cass mount
three horses, and taking a pack of hound dogs, they begin their pursuit
of Tomey's Turl. When the dogs jump Tomey's Turl and flush him
out, the dogs, happy to see an old friend, jump all over him, licking
his face and happily disappearing with him into the woods. Cass comi-
cally concludes: "It wasn't any race at all."

Uncle Buck wants to use Mr. Hubert's fyce (a very small, feisty
dog) to find the hounds – wherever Tomey's Turl has hidden them –
but Mr. Hubert changes the subject and maintains that all they have
to do in order to catch Tomey's Turl is to wait until midnight and
then walk up to Tennie's house. Mr. Hubert is willing to bet $500.00
to prove that he is right. Uncle Buck accepts the bet because he thinks
that he can catch Tomey's Turl well before midnight and be home.

The wager is made, and they wait until one of the Negroes brings
Uncle Buck a little bob-tailed black fyce, a fresh bottle of whiskey,
and, as though this "quest" for Tomey's Turl were like an Arthurian
deed, Uncle Buck is given a piece of red ribbon from around Miss
Sophonsiba's neck, a ribbon which Uncle Buck holds "like it was a
little water moccasin." The fyce finds the hounds just before sundown – all eleven dogs are shut up in a ten-foot-square cotton-house.
Again, the $500.00 bet is renewed: Uncle Buck boasts that Mr. Hubert
won't "catch that nigger in Tennie's cabin at midnight tonight" because
he, Uncle Buck, will have caught Tomey's Turl, and they will all be
home by midnight.

Using the fyce and the smell from Tomey's Turl's coat, Uncle Buck
tracks Tomey's Turl unsuccessfully until it is midnight. Then, even
Uncle Buck gives up and starts back toward the house, "the fyce riding
too now, in front of the nigger on the mule."

Suddenly, however, the fyce gives a yelp, leaps down, and "trees"
Tomey's Turl in Tennie's house. But when Uncle Buck sends Cass
around to pound on the back door, Tomey's Turl runs out the front
door, knocking Uncle Buck down, running "right clean over him," but
catching him (Uncle Buck) and dragging him along for ten feet before
"he threw him away and went on."

Uncle Buck's only "injury" is a broken whiskey bottle in his back pocket, and only when he knows for certain that whiskey and not blood is on the back of his pants, do he and Cass feel their way upstairs to an opened bedroom with a supposedly empty bed in it. Uncle Buck removes his boots and trousers and "roll[s] into the bed. That was when Miss Sophonsiba sat up on the other side of Uncle Buck and gave the first scream."

In the overall view of this section, we move from the "fox hunt," which is all in innocent fun, with the only damage being ashes mixed in with breakfast, to the "hunt" for Tomey's Turl, who is headed toward the Beauchamps to see Tennie, one of their slaves. In this second chase, or "hunt," which is presented in the same terms as that of a real fox hunt, note that matrimony becomes involved. Tomey's Turl wants to marry Tennie, but neither of the white masters will consent.

The "hunt" for Tomey's Turl leads Uncle Buck to the Beauchamps, where the first wager is made between Hubert Beauchamp and Uncle Buck concerning: (1) how long it will take Uncle Buck to catch Tomey's Turl, and (2) the method to be used. Here at the Beauchamps, the third "hunt" is initiated—that is, Sophonsiba's hunt for a husband. However, despite the fact that the dogs are good at hunting the fox, the "hunt" is done all in good fun, and although Uncle Buck is good at hunting Tomey's Turl (with no physical harm intended), it is Miss Sophonsiba who wins the prize as *the best of all hunters* (better even than the dogs or Uncle Buck), for she grimly pursues without relinquishment the harrowed Uncle Buck until she "trees" him in bed. Miss Sophonsiba is the most predacious, the most guileful, and the most relentless of all the hunters, and she is the *only one* who achieves her goal, even though her "win" is later lost for her because of her inept, poker-playing brother, Mr. Hubert.

Thus, from the "fox hunt" to the "hunt" for Tomey's Turl to Miss Sophonsiba's "hunt" for Uncle Buck as her husband, the stakes become more dangerous and more competitive, as each of the "hunted" becomes more desirous of escaping. But seemingly, both the fox and the dog *know* that the stakes are for innocent amusement, and, likewise, both Tomey's Turl and Uncle Buck *know* that Tomey's Turl will not be hurt. Both of these "hunts" are more a ritualized game than anything else. But with Miss Sophonsiba, the stakes are both dangerous *and* final, and if innocence plays a part in *her* hunt, it is used as an unsuspecting trap in the form of an open bedroom door.

We should now return to the opening of the story to discover more clearly that the hunt for Tomey's Turl is *not* a frenzied, desperate "hunt," in the tradition of the white slave master who is tracking down a runaway slave. In fact, while it is not mentioned in this story, the reader should be aware that Uncle Buck and Uncle Buddy do not believe in slavery; they have been practicing a type of manumission, wherein the slaves can free themselves.

With this in mind, the "hunt" – that is, the chase, really – takes on a different perspective. It becomes a ritualized performance, one which occurs at least twice a year. It is, in fact, a performance so ritualized that before embarking on it, Uncle Buck even *pretends* haste; he says, "'Tomey's Turl has broke out again. Give me and Cass some breakfast *quick* [my italics]. We might just barely catch him." Note that Uncle Buck takes time out to have his breakfast; he is too old to go hunting without breakfast. And note too that he also takes time out to find and don his necktie, an event in itself which attests to the ritualized aspect of this hunt. The tie, of course, *is necessary*; it is an important detail because Uncle Buck is a part of the "back-country aristocracy," and he *knows* that he will be encountering the aristocratic "man-hunter," in the person of Miss Sophonsiba Beauchamp, and thus, he must be properly attired, with his tie on.

Clearly, one of the underlying, comic implications here involves the "so-called" haste, or the need to "re-capture" Tomey's Turl. The "hunt" is emphatically *not* a "slave-hunt"; it has absolutely nothing to do with Tomey's Turl's so-called "escape" – in fact, within the larger construction of the McCaslin history, it is essential to remember that Uncle Buck and Uncle Buddy have moved the "slaves" into the big house, where there are no screens, no window locks, nor glass on any of the windows, and, after the front door is locked, every one of the "slaves" proceeds to climb out the open windows and roam about at leisure, knowing that they have to be back in the "big house" by morning, when the doors are unlocked.

Consequently, the not-so-frantic haste to recapture Tomey's Turl is not at all a stereotype of a chase by a "slavemaster," a villain from *Uncle Tom's Cabin* chasing an innocent Eliza with vicious bloodhounds. In fact, note the comic effect when the hounds are *supposed* to capture Tomey's Turl; they do "tree" him, but then they jump up and around in joy and lick his face. Tomey's Turl and the dogs are old friends.

Clearly, the entire chase is to capture Tomey's Turl *before he reaches Warwick* — because then, Mr. Hubert Beauchamp will find him and will voluntarily return the runaway, at which time Mr. Hubert will bring along his sister, the unmarried Miss Sophonsiba, who will remain as a guest in Uncle Buck and Uncle Buddy's house for an indeterminate period of time. This has, in fact, happened. One time in the past, when Mr. Hubert was returning Tomey's Turl, he brought along Miss Sophonsiba. Then, early one morning, Mr. Hubert tried to"escape" back to his own home, leaving the unchaperoned Miss Sophonsiba alone and "unprotected" in the house of the two bachelors — whereupon, by the standards of the day, Miss Sophonsiba could complain that she was "somewhat compromised." Consequently, it is *absolutely essential* that Uncle Buck capture Tomey's Turl as quickly as possible so as to prevent Miss Sophonsiba from coming to his cabin for another "extended visit."

Furthermore, Uncle Buddy is also aware of the extreme danger involved in this hunt to recapture Tomey's Turl — not that Tomey's Turl is "dangerous," but Uncle Buck's inviolate bachelorhood *is* seriously threatened when he goes into "she-bear" country. (Note that Mr. Hubert uses this terminology in Part 3 of the story, when he explains to Uncle Buck how he has been caught by Miss Sophonsiba.) Accordingly, since Uncle Buddy fears for Uncle Buck's "safety" in Miss Sophonsiba's home, he makes young Cass promise "the minute anything begins to look wrong, you ride to hell back here and get me." This, of course, is *exactly* what young Cass does when Mr. Hubert beats Uncle Buck in their first poker game.

Part of the humor of the second type of "hunt" is that Faulkner uses the terminology of a real fox hunt in describing how the boy and the men track down Tomey's Turl: "I'll *circle* him through the woods and we will *bay* him at the creek ford. . . ." They also *set dogs* on Tomey's Turl so that they can *tree* him, or so that they can *flush* him before he *breaks cover,* and they *bait* him before he can *den.* (Note also that all the words of the hunt, or chase, are also later applied to Miss Sophonsiba's hunt for a husband.)

The use of the conventional, ritual words of a formalized fox hunt again emphasizes that this hunt is *not* a hunt wherein a white master hunts down an escaped slave with vicious intent. This fact alone sets apart both Uncle Buck and Tomey's Turl from the conventional society of the time (1859), which would have hunted down an escaped slave, using guns and bloodhounds. Even the hunt itself emphasizes how unconventional this pursuit really is: it is understood that Uncle Buck will catch Tomey's Turl with *only* his bare hands, and as noted above, the dogs *are* friendly and are in no way dangerous.

While reading Part 3 of "Was," if we remember that Uncle Buddy warned Cass to come fetch him *immediately*, as soon as something "looked wrong," it seems natural that Faulkner opens Part 3 with young Cass narrating how Uncle Buck was trapped ("treed") by Miss Sophonsiba and how Mr. Hubert was delighted that she had finally caught him. Uncle Buck tries to explain his innocence in being in Miss Sophonsiba's bed, that it is all an accident, but Mr. Hubert simply tells Uncle Buck to explain *that* to Miss Sophonsiba, whose voice can still be steadily heard somewhere in the house.

Mr. Hubert then explains the incident in terms of "the hunt": "You [Uncle Buck] come into bear-country and you knew the way back out. . . . But no. You had to crawl into the den and lay down by the bear. And whether you did or didn't know the bear was in it don't make any difference. . . . She's got you, 'Filus, and you know it. You run a hard race and you run a good one, but you skun the hen-house one time too many." Uncle Buck then refers to the five hundred dollars that Mr. Hubert bet – that is, Mr. Hubert bet Uncle Buck that he (Uncle Buck) would "catch" Tomey's Turl in Tennie's house *after dark*. And Uncle Buck bet that he (Uncle Buck) would "catch" Tomey's Turl *long before dark*. Therefore, Mr. Hubert lost the bet, and Uncle Buck wants the money. Furthermore, Uncle Buck maintains that even if there had been ten men at Tennie's cabin, Tomey's Turl would not have been captured. Uncle Buck and Mr. Hubert decide to settle things with a hand of poker: "Five hundred dollars against Sibbey [Sophonsiba]," and the winner is to buy the other one's slave for three hundred dollars – that is, "The lowest hand wins Sibbey and buys the niggers" – which is confusing because it is really *the loser who will get Sibbey*, but in gentlemen's terms, it is more *polite* to say that the person who gets Sibbey is a winner, rather than a loser, even though he has, in reality, just *lost the poker game* and is forced to take Sibbey, making him, unwillingly, the "winner."

When the poker hand is dealt and played, Mr. Hubert wins the hand, meaning that Uncle Buck has *lost* the hand, but that he has "won" Sibbey and the "right" to buy Tennie – all because he is the "loser" of the poker game but the winner of Miss Sophonsiba. And Uncle

Buck isn't romantically interested in Sibbey, and neither is he interested in buying Tennie.

It is soon after this that Uncle Buck awakens Cass and sends him on his pony to fetch Uncle Buddy. Later, after supper at Warwick, another poker game is arranged – this time between Uncle Buddy and Mr. Hubert. This time, the stakes are increased, as follows: if Mr. Hubert *wins* the hand, Uncle Buck marries Miss Sophonsiba without a dowry. If Mr. Hubert *loses* this hand, Uncle Buck goes free with the chastity of his bachelorhood unviolated, but Uncle Buck must *still* buy the slave Tennie for $300.00.

The two men call in someone to deal, and the game of Stud is dealt: Mr. Hubert has 3 three's, a king, and an ace showing, while Uncle Buddy has 2 two's, a four, a five, and a six showing. If Uncle Buddy's hidden card is a three (the last three in the deck), then Uncle Buddy wins. At this point, Uncle Buddy raises the wager by betting "them two niggers" against the "three hundred dollars" that Uncle Buck owes Mr. Hubert for "winning" (or losing, depending on who assesses the first poker game) earlier.

Upon consideration, Mr. Hubert asks *who* dealt the cards. The low light slowly reveals that it was Tomey's Turl who dealt, and at that revelation, Mr. Hubert passes, and thus, according to the original bet, Mr. Hubert loses and *still* has Miss Sophonsiba, but Uncle Buddy (and Uncle Buck) *have to buy* Tennie for Tomey's Turl.

In Part 3, then, the poker game is played for very high stakes – Uncle Buck's freedom, and Tennie and Tomey's Turl's future life together. Matrimony is involved in both instances. For Uncle Buck, matrimony is a dreaded kind of slavery, but for the "slaves," matrimony is their main objective – that is, they will have the *freedom* to enter into marriage. Consequently, since the betting will allow Tomey's Turl and Tennie to get married regardless of who wins, some readers are puzzled as to why Tomey's Turl is so intent upon Uncle Buddy's winning and why Tomey's Turl manipulates the dealing so as to *make sure* that Uncle Buck, the man *chasing him,* does indeed finally win.

Looking back, it should now be clear that throughout the entire "hunt," Tomey's Turl has the upper hand, or is at least in charge of the *strategy* of the "hunt" and in control of the *manipulation* of the poker game. After all, even though it is never mentioned during this particular story, Uncle Buck is, in fact, "hunting" *his own half-brother.* Tomey's Turl is old McCaslin's son *(and grandson),* which explains why Mr. Hubert calls him that "damn half-white McCaslin" (which is not wholly accurate because Tomey's Turl would be three-fourths white – that is, a quadroon).

Consequently, it should now be clear why Tomey's Turl has arranged for Uncle Buddy to win; that way, Uncle Buddy will have to buy Tennie and Mr. Hubert won't have to buy Tomey's Turl. Tomey's Turl *is a McCaslin,* and he wants his bride on his father's land (a part of which he has already inherited, even though he has not claimed it). And even though his black descendants will take on Tennie's last name and become Beauchamps, at present, Tomey's Turl is still a McCaslin.

Furthermore, whereas Mr. Hubert recognizes and approves of the institution of slavery, Uncle Buck and Uncle Buddy are *opposed* to slavery. Tomey's Turl would not allow himself to be bought by Mr. Hubert, and he must arrange things so that Uncle Buck and Uncle Buddy (his half-brothers) will *have to buy Tennie*; that way, Tomey's Turl can marry Tennie and live on the McCaslin plantation.

In reviewing the story, almost everything is, or can be, seen as a light-hearted *ritualized game* being played by Uncle Buddy, Uncle Buck, and Cass in innocent fun. For Miss Sophonsiba and Tomey's Turl, however, the "game" is not taken lightly. Faulkner's interplay with irony and humor is masterful.

The concluding, short fourth section shows the return home; Cass, Uncle Buddy, and Tennie (who is now a part of the McCaslins) are riding in the wagon, and Tomey's Turl is riding the mule. At home, Old Moses (the dog) climbs in the crate with the fox, who goes right through the back of the crate, followed by Old Moses and all of the dogs until the fox (Sothey) goes "scrabbling up the lean-pole onto the roof." Uncle Buddy is upset, but Uncle Buck only wants his breakfast because it *seems* as though he's "been away from home a whole damn month."

At the end of the tale, the dogs have chased the fox, Uncle Buck has chased Tomey's Turl, and Miss Sophonsiba has chased Uncle Buck, and all have been unsuccessful. *Only* Tomey's Turl is a winner – he has captured Tennie, his future bride.

THE FIRE AND THE HEARTH

Although such a distinguished critic as Cleanth Brooks refers to this story as "a long story that is surely one of Faulkner's finest," most readers find it to be the most diffuse and the least unified in the volume. Some of this seeming disunity, however, can be partly accounted for by the fact that in this story, Faulkner combines two previously published stories ("A Point of Law," published in *Collier's,* June 22, 1940, and "Gold Is Not Always," published in *The American Mercury,* November, 1940. Both of these earlier stories, dealing with Lucas Beauchamp, are now available as separate stories in *Uncollected Stories of William Faulkner*).

Faulkner fashioned these two separate stories into the first two sections of "The Fire and the Hearth," and then he added additional, unpublished material concerning the Beauchamp-McCaslin-Edmonds relationship, as well as previously unpublished material dealing with the desire of Molly, Lucas' wife, for a divorce.

For those who expect to read the entire *Go Down, Moses* as a unified novel, this particular story presents an initial difficulty – that is, the previous story, "Was," focused on a central character simply referred to as "he." But until Faulkner identifies the unknown "he" of "The Fire and the Hearth" as being Lucas Beauchamp, some readers might easily assume that this "he" is the *same* "he" as was referred to in the preceding story *unless* the reader had before him a general history of the McCaslin family, along with a genealogy.

In spite of this possible, initial confusion, however, "The Fire and the Hearth" is significantly related to the previous story by Faulkner's use of the same family, the same land, and the same themes. In fact, the critic Dirk Kuyk, Jr., assesses the story in this way: " 'The Fire and the Hearth' is a small-scale *Go Down, Moses.* As the tangled narration makes the book a wilderness, 'The Fire and the Hearth' is a thicket, smaller but just as dense."

For the sake of seeing this story in its largest concerns, it can perhaps be best divided as follows:

Chapter One:	Part 1 of this chapter presents the humorous conflict between Lucas Beauchamp (a *black* man who is a descendant of the *white* McCaslin family) and George Wilkins, his prospective *black* son-in-law, concerning the illegal distilling of corn whiskey.
	Part 2 of this chapter has a long digression into the past concerning Lucas Beauchamp's tense relationship with Zack Edmonds over the duties of Lucas' wife, Molly.
Chapter Two:	This chapter begins the story of Lucas' search for "buried treasure," and it focuses primarily on Lucas' outsmarting a big city mine-detector salesman, using the oldest ruse known – that is, "salting a mine," deliberately planting some money in a place where an unsuspecting person will accidentally find it and think that there *has* to be more money hidden there.
Chapter Three:	This chapter presents Molly's desire to divorce Lucas after forty-three years of marriage because of Lucas' psychotic (or neurotic) determination to find buried treasure – at the expense of all other considerations, especially those of family concerns and ties.
	Section 1 of this chapter has a digression concerning the inheritance that old Carothers McCaslin left to Lucas' father (Tomey's Turl of "Was"), who refused to accept it. It was thus passed down to Lucas and his brother (Tennie's Jim, or James Beauchamp) and their sister (Fonsiba). Lucas, upon coming of age, demands his share of the inheritance.
	The above digression is followed by another digression concerning Lucas' son, Henry, and Zack's son, Carothers (Roth), both of whom were born at approximately the same time and whose childhood friendship with each other remained strong until racial issues intruded upon, and forever changed, the relationship between the two white and black *foster-brothers*.

Despite the fact that all of these concerns *seem* to be disjointed, they are all part of, and are connected with, the central plot-line of this story and the other stories in this book because they *all* deal with family ties, inheritance, racial issues, and the relationship of man to the land.

Basically, "The Fire and the Hearth" presents Lucas Beauchamp's domestic state at a time when it is being threatened by his greed for buried treasure. The title of the story, "The Fire and the Hearth," is symbolic of the relationship that Lucas once had with his wife. Together, Lucas and Molly built the fire in the hearth on the first day of their marriage, and it has burned there winter and summer for forty-three years. During these years, Lucas has faithfully tended to his farming, respecting the land and the fruit it produced. Until now, he has yielded to no temptations in any form – that is, until the events of this story, which begin when Lucas finds a gold coin. Then he is rapidly transformed into almost another person by his ruthlessness in trying to eliminate a competitor who is a threat to his bootlegging enterprises.

Lucas' overwhelming greed is manifested in his frantic desire to find buried treasure. The search, it is quickly obvious, is destroying the foundation of his marriage, and there is also an intimation that the qualities associated with Lucas' greed for buried money are the consequences of his *white blood.* Only when Molly, his wife, is suing for divorce at the end of the story does Lucas realize that "man has got three score and ten years on this earth, the Book says." It is then that Lucas gives up his search for buried treasure; he realizes that he doesn't have much time left.

During the present time of these stories (1941), Lucas is sixty-seven years old, and as is often typical of old people, Lucas will reminisce about many aspects of the past. At the beginning of "The Fire and the Hearth," the focus of this story is on the present: Lucas is enraged that he must *singlehandedly* hide his still. He must dismantle it and then transport it away all by himself. He has operated the still for over twenty years without Carothers (Roth) Edmonds (the white owner of the McCaslin lands) ever knowing about it. But now Lucas is making plans to get rid of his competition by having the sheriff discover, or gain knowledge of, George Wilkins' still – even though George is Lucas' prospective black son-in-law.

But before he does that, Lucas must hide his own still so that the sheriff, when searching for George Wilkins' still, will not find Lucas' still. Lucas has *nothing personal* against George Wilkins – it is just that George is careless and foolish and will eventually, Lucas thinks, ruin the entire bootlegging operation because of his ineptness. Further-more, Wilkins is intruding upon Lucas' established territory, and Wilkins' childish and amateurish attitude toward bootlegging is bound to be bad for everyone: "And [Lucas] not only didn't want a fool for a son-in-law, he didn't intend to have a fool living on the same place he lived on." It is better, Lucas decides, if George were to spend "some time" in the state penitentiary at Parchman rather than endanger Lucas' well-established bootlegging operation.

Thus, the two seemingly divergent strands of "The Fire and the Hearth" – the story of George Wilkins and the distillery, and the story of the buried treasure – are brought together in this opening section of Chapter One when Lucas, while searching for a place to hide his still, discovers a single gold coin in an old buried churn, and this leads to his almost-maniacal search for buried treasure.

The discovery of the gold coin makes it absolutely necessary that George Wilkins *must* be gotten rid of *immediately* so as to keep the sheriff and other people from snooping about and possibly discovering the buried treasure. However, as Lucas finishes burying his still in "the Indian mound," he is suddenly aware of another presence, and upon investigation, he discovers the unmistakable, bare footprints of his daughter, Nat, who has been observing all of her father's myster-ious activities. (It will be much later in the story, though, before Nat is implicated in the discovery of Lucas' still because of her close obser-vation of her father's nighttime digging.)

In order to get rid of George Wilkins, Lucas goes to the plantation house to tell Carothers (Roth) Edmonds that George Wilkins is distill-ing and selling bootleg whiskey on plantation property; he is sure that Roth will report this information to the sheriff. "The report would have to come from Edmonds, the white man, because to the sheriff, Lucas was just another nigger and both the sheriff and Lucas knew it, although only one of them knew that to Lucas, the sheriff was a red-neck without any reason for pride in his forbears nor hope for it in his descendants."

When Roth appears on the porch, Faulkner delays the action of the plot and inserts a long, involved digression. Lucas is reminded of the circumstances surrounding Roth's birth. Roth's mother had come into labor during a heavy flood, and Molly, Lucas' wife, delivered the child, but when complications set in, Lucas risked his own life by swimming across the flooded river to fetch the doctor for Roth's mother, but by the time he returned, Roth's mother was already dead, and Molly, who had just given birth to her son Henry, remained at the plantation house to nurse both her son and baby Roth. Six months passed, and during this time, Lucas lived alone, keeping the fire going in the hearth. But one day, he suddenly (and unaccountably) became furious. He felt that his honor had been infringed upon, and so he went to Zack Edmonds and demanded Molly be sent home, saying, "I reckon you thought I wouldn't take her back."

This statement obviously implies that Lucas thought that Zack Edmonds had been using Molly as his mistress, an idea which would fit into Lucas' concept of the entire McCaslin brood, going back to old Carothers McCaslin's relations with the slave Eunice and with Lucas' grandmother, Tomasina. To Lucas, Zack was just another old Carothers McCaslin who would sleep with any of the black slaves. Later, however, Lucas was angry that Zack did *not* sleep with Molly; in a way, the fact that Zack did not use Molly as a mistress seemed to be an insult. Thus, Lucas was determined to get revenge, and he showed his contempt for Zack by saying sarcastically, *"And that's a man."*

When Molly did return home, she brought the white child (Roth) with her, and when Lucas noticed his wife suckling the white child, he became incensed and was convinced that he had been betrayed (or cuckolded). Lucas anticipated his revenge by waiting for Zack to come to his house. He says, "I went to Zack Edmonds' house and asked him for my wife. Let him come to my house and ask me for his son."

When Zack did not come, Lucas' desire for revenge was not satis-fied – instead, he planned a direct confrontation with Zack, even though it might mean that he, Lucas, would be lynched afterward. This decision resulted in a tense, physical struggle between the two men. First, they had a hand-to-hand combat involving a gun; then they battled with a razor, and finally, they fought with their bare hands. This is a struggle which would not be understandable in terms of Southern racial attitudes if we, the readers, were not aware of the *family blood ties* that exist between Lucas (a mulatto) and Zack (a white). That is, this whole situation would be unthinkable for a typical

Southern black man of that time and a typical white man, but these two men both share a common ancestor – old Carothers McCaslin.

In fact, Faulkner tells us, Lucas and Zack "had known [each other] from infancy . . . had lived until they were both grown almost as brothers lived. They had fished and hunted together, they had learned to swim in the same water, they had eaten at the same table in the white boy's kitchen and in the cabin of the Negro's mother; they had slept under the same blanket before a fire in the woods."

This relationship alone is unique; it is a *violation* of the Southern societal relationship between blacks and whites. But since this relationship *does exist*, Zack is aware of just how much Lucas feels that his honor has been tampered with, and Zack is also aware of the seriousness of the struggle between them. He also knows that Lucas is a man of honor, and he knows that Lucas *could* have slipped in and killed Zack in the darkness, but he didn't. Instead, Lucas waited until morning, and then he told Zack to "get your gun from under the pillow." Lucas also threw away his razor (a common weapon for black men at that time), and the struggle was finally fought with bare hands, neither man yielding until Zack made a leap for the gun on the bed.

During the struggle, Lucas was able to fire the gun into Zack's side, but the gun misfired, and suddenly, all of Lucas' fury, anger, and passion was exhausted, and he left, still not knowing whether or not Zack had slept with Molly. Returning home, Lucas accepted, without rancor, the fact that Molly was nursing both the black child *and* the white child.

After this long digression, section 3 of Chapter One returns to the front porch, where Lucas is telling Roth about George Wilkins' still and also about the whiskey hid under the floor in Wilkins' kitchen. Lucas is sure that Roth will inform the sheriff, which he does.

The next morning, Lucas' plan backfires, however, when he awakens and finds George Wilkins' still in his back yard and the quart-sized cans, as well as the five-gallon cans, of distilled whiskey standing on his porch. His daughter, Nat, who was watching her father's nighttime maneuverings, has now put her father in a compromising position so as to protect George, who is already (secretly) her husband.

Before Lucas can do anything, however, the sheriff and his deputies arrive, and they take Lucas, George, and Nat into town to the courthouse for arraignment. During the legal process, Lucas learns that a "kin-person" can't testify against a "kin-folk," and since Nat *can't* testify against Lucas, but can testify against George (so everyone thinks), and George *can* testify against Lucas, Lucas changes his mind about Nat and George marrying. Nat, however, won't have anything to do with "marrying George," she says, until *someone* (meaning Lucas) builds a new back porch, buys her a cook stove, and digs a well so that she won't have to walk a mile and a half to tote water. Her refusals are directed *to Lucas,* whom she wants to provide the money for these items.

Later at the trial, after Lucas has found out that Nat and George are married, he produces a document which shows that Nat and George Wilkins were married *last October,* after the cotton was harvested; therefore, Nat *can't testify* against anyone – neither against Lucas nor against George – and so the judge finally dismisses everyone.

In section 4 of Chapter One, Nat is complaining to Lucas that George has not bought the stove yet. Nor has he started on the porch, nor on the well, and furthermore, he has already spent the money that Lucas gave them. So Lucas goes to George Wilkins' place and inspects the new still that George bought with the money which Lucas gave him. At this point, Lucas finally accepts George as his new apprentice in the art of distilling bootleg whiskey.

Some of the details of this chapter of the story might seem confusing, especially those relating to George and Nat's marriage date and Nat's trip to Vicksburg. But according to the document presented to the judge in court, Nat and George Wilkins were married at the end of the harvest *last* October (remember the time of the *present* story is during spring planting). Yet, apparently, Nat would not go to live in George's house until he had a new stove, a new back porch, and a well in the back yard so that she wouldn't have to walk a mile and a half to tote water.

Thus, we now realize why Nat was following, or tailing, Lucas during all of his nightly wanderings. She was trying to find some way to force her father to realize that she and George *should* be married so that she couldn't testify against *either one* of them about the illegal bootlegging and the illegal stills. Nat *knew* her father had the money to buy the things which she wanted, but she had to use subterfuges to get her way.

When Lucas finally realized the need of having Nat and George married, he arranged for Nat to go to Vicksburg. But when Nat (who was already married to George) announced that she wouldn't marry George until she got her way, she forced Lucas to agree *both* to the marriage *and* to the stove, the porch, and the well. In other words, all of Nat's and George's machinations are done solely to trap Lucas in a situation where he would not only have to approve of the marriage which *had already* taken place secretly, but he would be forced to provide the needed items for George's house – improvements which Nat demands. Lucas' plans to trap George are reversed, and we see Lucas being trapped by George and Nat into letting them have their own way, and furthermore, George ends up being *not only* Lucas' son-in-law, but also a partner in the bootlegging enterprise.

Chapter Two of "The Fire and the Hearth" returns to Lucas' overwhelming obsession to find the buried treasure in the old Indian mound where he discovered a single gold piece (at the beginning of Chapter One) while he was trying to bury his still. In pursuit of his goal, Lucas ordered a "divining machine" from a St. Louis firm, reputed to be able to detect buried treasure. Now, a salesman has arrived to collect the three hundred dollars owed on the machine. Lucas, not wanting to risk his savings, tries unsuccessfully to con Roth Edmonds into paying for the machine, which Roth adamantly refuses to do. Lucas then "borrows" a valuable mule belonging to Roth and gives it to the man from St. Louis as "security" for the divining machine, promising to buy back the mule after they find the buried treasure.

When Roth finds the mule missing, he knows immediately that Lucas has taken it, and so he tracks Lucas down and orders him to return the mule. Lucas cannot do so. He tells the man from St. Louis that he needs more time with the machine, and the salesman tells Lucas that it will cost him twenty-five dollars a night to rent the machine – until the mule business is cleared up. Lucas is then forced to use another ruse.

He sends George Wilkins into town to get fifty silver dollar pieces, which he buries in the orchard, and then he tells the salesman about a secret letter which he "misread." When they discover the buried fifty dollars, he and the salesman argue about whom it belongs to; then they make an arrangement so that the salesman will get *half the money* – in return for the bill of sale for the mule and acknowledgment of Lucas' possession of the divining machine.

Three days later, Roth comes to Lucas' house and discovers that Lucas has been up every night watching the salesman hunt for buried treasure with Lucas' machine, which Lucas now rents to the salesman for twenty-five dollars a night. Last night, however, the salesman did *not* show up, so Lucas assumes that they are rid of him.

Essentially, Chapter Two does not vary much from Faulkner's original short story. Its basic plot narration, in anecdotal fashion, or in the fashion of "Old Southwest Humor," yields the essential value of the story. For example, we see the "city slicker" salesman trying to sell a worthless gimmick to an unsuspecting "country bumpkin," who will soon be the butt of a joke. But then the tables are turned, and the city slicker is forced to retreat to the safety of his city, leaving the country bumpkin, in the person of Lucas, as the victor. These reversals make for good comic reading. At first, Lucas rents the divining machine, and then he gains the upper hand through using the old ruse of the salted mine; as a result, the salesman finds himself renting his own machine from Lucas and paying him much more than the money which Lucas used to salt the orchard. Throughout all of these proceedings, Lucas never takes the salesman anywhere near the old Indian mound, where he actually found the single gold coin.

Chapter Three of "The Fire and the Hearth" returns to Lucas' treasure hunting. Apparently enough time has elapsed to show that Lucas and George Wilkins have been spending every night at the Indian mound searching for buried treasure and that Molly has had to do all the chores, chores which she wouldn't mind doing if Lucas were, in fact, sick in body, but now she thinks that Lucas is sick in the mind. Therefore, she comes to the plantation office to ask Roth Edmonds to get her a divorce.

When Roth assures Molly that Lucas will soon quit his search, Molly explains that she is afraid that he *might* find buried treasure, which would be a violation of God's command and that God would then punish him for removing it. As Molly explains it: "Because God say, 'What's rendered to My earth, it belongs to Me unto I resurrect it. And let him or her touch it, and beware!'" Roth then promises to talk to Lucas, even though Molly feels it will do no good.

After Molly leaves, Roth recalls certain events concerning the family relationships between the McCaslins, the Edmondses, and the Beauchamps. Lucas, Roth recalls, is *not only* the oldest living person on the plantation, but Lucas is *also* the closest descendant to old Carothers McCaslin himself, who left an inheritance to his three-fourths white son, Tomey's Turl, who never availed himself of the sum, which was then passed on to his three living children – James, who disappeared before coming of age; Fonsiba, who married and moved to Arkansas (where Uncle Ike, then a young man, followed her and deposited her third of the legacy in a bank); and Lucas, more black than white. But Lucas has remained on the plantation, living on a plot of land in the center, set aside for the descendants of Tomey's Turl, for as long as these descendants want to live on it or farm it.

When Lucas turned twenty-one, he appeared before Ike to demand the legacy due to him and also to have James Beauchamp's portion transferred to his (Lucas') name for safekeeping. Lucas was persuaded to keep the amount in the bank, and he agreed to do so, after he was convinced that the bank was honest and responsible, even to a black man.

Roth continues his digression, remembering that Lucas decided to stay on the plantation and married a town woman. Then Roth recalls how Cass Edmonds (Roth's grandfather) built a cabin for Lucas and his wife, and how, when Roth was born, Henry Beauchamp, Lucas' son, was born at the same time, and since Roth's mother died, he and Henry were both nursed and tended to by Molly so that they grew up almost as brothers. They both ate at the same table and slept in either the same bed, or else on the same pallet.

But one day, when Roth was seven years old, and he and Henry were preparing to go to bed, Roth revolted from sleeping in the same bed: "One day the old curse of his fathers, the old haughty ancestral pride based not on any value but on an accident of geography, stemmed not from courage and honor but from wrong and shame, descended on him." After his refusal to let Henry share the same bed, Roth realized the utter shame he felt, even though he could not admit the shame.

After that, "they [Roth and Henry] never slept in the same room again and never again ate at the same table." Roth was so ashamed of his actions that he avoided Henry for a month. Then one day, he boldly entered the cabin, where he announced that he would eat with Henry and his family that night. The Beauchamps accepted him gladly, but they also recognized the change that had taken place: "The table was set in the kitchen where it always was, and Molly stood at the stove drawing the biscuits out as she always stood, but Lucas was not there and there was just one chair, one plate, his glass of milk beside it, the platter heaped with untouched chicken, and even as he sprang back, gasping, for an instant blind as the room rushed and swam, Henry was turning toward the door to go out of it. 'Are you ashamed to eat when I eat?' he [Roth] cried. Henry paused, turning his head a little to speak in the voice slow and without heat: 'I ain't shamed of nobody,' he said peacefully. 'Not even me.'"

It is at this reminiscence that Roth again contemplates his father's and his own relationship with Lucas, and he finally comes to realize that Lucas and his father once fought over the same woman, and that Lucas was the winner.

Returning to the present time, Roth Edmonds tries to talk sense to Lucas about the divorce, but Lucas is stubborn and keeps asserting, "I'm the man here. I'm the one to say in my house." Angrily, Roth demands that Lucas give up the divining machine, and then he leaves. This is on a Saturday.

On Monday, Roth hears that Molly has been missing since early Sunday. Upon searching, they find Molly nearly dead, lying face down in the swamp with the divining machine beside her. She had hoped to show Lucas how absurd his search was, and as a result, she almost killed herself from exhaustion. When Roth sees her prostrate body, he promises to get Molly a divorce.

At the court house, as the proceedings for the divorce are about to be finalized, Lucas suddenly appears and announces that they, he and Molly, do not want a divorce. As he and Molly leave the court house, Lucas buys Molly some hard candy.

In section 4 of Chapter Three of "The Fire and the Hearth," Lucas tells Roth to get rid of the machine. Even though he still believes that buried treasure does exist, Lucas realizes that God has given him "three score and ten years on this earth," and at age sixty-seven, he figures that he just doesn't have time enough left to find the treasure. The story concludes, then, with the fire in the hearth still burning, representing the fact that Lucas has now regained his sanity.

Earlier, we noted that one critic stated that this story seems to have a "tangled narration." After closely examining the story, however, one can deal with certain aspects of the so-called tangled narration which sometimes puzzles readers. For example, when some of the townspeople are amused at Lucas' and Uncle Ike's being seen together at the bank, we (the readers) must remember that there *are* family ties between the *black* Beauchamps and the *white* Edmondses; both are descended from old *white* Carothers McCaslin. Many of the townspeople are not aware of this fact, however, and many readers are not

48

aware of this either, unless a basic knowledge of the family is available (see McCaslin Genealogy). Also, we must remember that part of Roth's concern over Molly results from his viewing her as *the only mother* that he ever had.

Likewise, while this story deals essentially with Lucas Beauchamp, there seem to be many Lucases in this story. There is:

(1) the Lucas of the first part of the story, who is bent on getting rid of George Wilkins by informing against a *black* to the *white* establishment. Then there is:

(2) the Lucas who, as a young man, was bent upon revenge against his white kinsman, Zack, who "compromised Lucas' honor" (so Lucas *thought*). There is also:

(3) this same Lucas who acted with a strict code of honor when he confronted Zack, by waiting until daylight and then giving Zack ample opportunity to defend himself. Then we also have:

(4) a Lucas who is so imbued with a sense of personal honor that when he feels that this honor has been infringed upon, he is overcome with a terrible fury. And when Roth tries to get Lucas to quit hunting for gold, we have yet another Lucas,

(5) a Lucas who is a strong, domineering male, who asserts his masculine prerogative that *he* is a *man*; he is a Lucas who has an almost primitive lust for power, yet in his search for the buried treasure, we see

(6) a Lucas who has lost his basic common sense, a man who is foolish, childish, petulant, and domineering. Then there is

(7) the Lucas who is filled with a kind of ancestor worship for old white Carothers McCaslin, himself a man who, of course, was *not* an honorable person. And finally, there is

(8) the Lucas who is tender in his final concern for Molly, as he buys her some "hard" candy so that she can enjoy sucking on it since she doesn't have any teeth.

In conclusion, since Faulkner covered so much time, both in the chronological time of the story and in the combining of different stories with different objectives, it is somewhat difficult to formulate a clear picture of the person of Lucas.

PANTALOON IN BLACK

As many critics have pointed out, "Pantaloon in Black" has no, or only a tenuous, relation to the rest of the stories in *Go Down, Moses*. The readers or critics who attempt to force all of these stories into a unified and thematic novel go to extreme lengths to justify the inclusion of this story. As pointed out elsewhere, the original title was *Go Down, Moses and Other Stories,* and only when the book was reissued in 1949 did Faulkner drop the "and Other Stories" from the title.

Faulkner himself, however, referred to the book as a novel, and this reference has caused some readers and critics to look for strained and forced connections where there are none. For example, whereas the other stories deal with the lives of various descendants of Lucius Quintus Carothers McCaslin, neither Rider nor his wife, Mannie, nor his uncle nor his aunt have any connection with any member of that family. The only connections are that (1) Rider rents his cabin from Roth Edmonds, and (2) Rider, like Lucas in the preceding story, builds a fire in the hearth on his wedding day. But neither connection contributes to the importance of "Pantaloon in Black" as a short story. Essentially, it is best to consider this story in terms of its individual worth and not concern oneself with its relation, thematic or otherwise, with the rest of the stories in this volume.

Essentially, this story illustrates the white man's failure to perceive the black man's infinite capacity for love and the depth of the black man's commitment and devotion to his family.

The story is divided into two sections. The first section presents Rider as a central figure. Every detail of the narrative follows Rider's thoughts and actions. The second section presents Rider from the white deputy's perspective. It shows us the white man's perplexed attempt to explain Rider's actions – actions which remain incomprehensible to the white deputy and to most white people.

The first section opens at the funeral of Rider's wife, Mannie. They were married only six months, and during that time, Rider put aside his drinking, his carousing, his gambling, and his wild living – all for the sake of Mannie's love; and now that Mannie is dead, Rider is inconsolable. He is a large man ("He was better than two hundred pounds"), and in the opening scene, in a frenzied search for consolation, he grabs a shovel and frantically tries to help bury his wife. He refuses to go home with his aunt who raised him, and against the advice of his friends who feel that Mannie is "wawkin yit" (that is, her spirit it still walking), Rider heads for the cabin where he and Mannie lived before her death.

As Rider feeds the dog and eats some cold food himself, the dog begins to howl, and Mannie's spirit appears, "standing in the door, looking at him." He calls to her gently so as not to frighten her (in fact, he waits until his voice is calm so as to make sure he doesn't frighten her), but "as soon as he moved, she began to fade. . . . 'Wait,' he said, talking as sweet as he had ever heard his voice speak to a woman: 'Den lemme go wid you, honey.' But she was going. She was going fast now. . . ."

He discards his cold supper and heads to the sawmill where he works; there he performs violent and incredible feats of strength. At sundown, he goes to a white bootlegger, buys a jug of whiskey and drinks heavily, but he cannot alleviate his grief. Then he visits his old aunt, who offers him solace in prayer, which he rejects, and then he ends up in a crooked dice game run by a crooked white man. When Rider confronts the white man for cheating and makes him drop the extra loaded dice, the white man (named Birdsong) pulls a gun on Rider, who quickly cuts the white man's throat.

Throughout this first section, Faulkner presents a picture of a simple and primitive man possessed of colossal strength who can find no way to assuage his inconsolable grief. Like other Faulknerian characters (for example, Jewel in *As I Lay Dying*), Rider is a man of action who can express his grief only through acts which seem primitive to the white man, who cannot understand how a black man could, first of all, even feel such an intensity of emotion, and *then,* attempt to express his suffering in such incomprehensible behavior.

In addition to suggesting Rider's grief through his actions, Faulkner also shows us Rider's reaction to his wife's apparition in the poignant "wawkin scene," in which Mannie seems to appear first to the dog and then to Rider himself. We note Rider's deep devotion first in his deep concern that his voice might frighten her and then in his total acceptance of her. His first and foremost concern is that he will *not* frighten her away, and as she begins to fade from sight, he pleads,

"Den lemme go wid you, honey." By this plea, we know that Rider finds no value in his life and will not be concerned about his own life or welfare.

Part 2 of the story is narrated by the deputy sheriff, as he talks to his wife. She is completely insensitive to the events which totally baffle the deputy. Since the death of Birdsong, the crooked dice-dealer, Rider has been arrested, jailed, and then lynched by members of the Birdsong family. The deputy finds Rider's actions incomprehensible – incomprehensible because he sees Rider not as an individual, but as a "damn nigger" whose actions do not fit into his preconceived notions of how a black man *should* act. For the white man, any gigantic two-hundred-pound, six-foot black man capable of great feats of physical prowess could not *possibly* possess the sensitivity to grieve deeply over the death of his young black wife.

For example, to the white man, a typical black person would have used the opportunity of his wife's death to take off from work for at least a day. But does Rider grieve? According to the white deputy, Rider was "the biggest and busiest man at the funeral." Likewise, the fact that Rider gets drunk and gets into a fight are indications to the deputy that Rider is insensitive and ignorant. Blacks, the deputy says, "ain't human . . . when it comes to normal human feelings and sentiments of human beings, they might just as well be a damn herd of wild buffaloes."

What the white deputy can't understand is that Rider is *not* "just a black"; he is a *human being,* filled with deep grief, and he is using his great strength to literally bring about his own death. Even when he tears the door off the jail, he does not try to escape. Life without his wife has *no meaning* for Rider, and the white man cannot understand this incredible story of individualized love and grief. As the title suggests, the black man's face is a facade that hides forever the depth of his inconsolable grief from the callous white man.

THE OLD PEOPLE

Many people in their enthusiasm for "The Bear" have overlooked the excellence of "The Old People." In fact, one of Faulkner's best critics, Cleanth Brooks, in his *William Faulkner: The Yoknapatawpha Country*, devotes fifteen pages to a discussion of "The Bear," but he dismisses "The Old People" in one brief paragraph, saying: "The plot element here is slight, so slight that one is tempted to regard "The Old People" not so much a story as merely a lovingly elaborated character sketch of the old hunter Sam Fathers . . . who becomes Isaac's mentor."

Yet, this story is thoroughly appreciated by many critics and anthologists, and even though this story covers some of the same ground as "The Bear" does, and even though both stories were originally published separately, a knowledge of this story seems essential (or highly beneficial) for a full appreciation of "The Bear."

For example, Sam Fathers occupies a prominent position in this story; he achieves his greatest stature as one of Faulkner's memorable characters here; it is in this story that Sam becomes a living memorial to the virtues of a life dedicated to the wilderness. In contrast, Sam's importance in "The Bear" seems to be substantially lessened unless we know the qualities which are attributed to him in "The Old People." Likewise, the theme of civilization encroaching upon and destroying the values of the wilderness are first presented in "The Old People." But, unlike Brooks, who feels that Sam Fathers is the main justification for this story, most critics see the central intent of this story as Isaac's initiation into the life of a hunter, into manhood, and into the spiritual mysteries of the wilderness. In fact, the entire story is imbued with the mythic, the supernatural, and the religious.

Accordingly, the story opens in a mythic, or biblical, style: "At first there was nothing. There was the faint, cold, steady rain, the gray and constant light of the late November dawn, with the voices of the hounds converging somewhere in it and toward them."

Certainly, this is an effective opening, but we are not aware that this is the *climax of the story* until we again read this passage later in the story. This passage, however, is the key to the story, and it contains this critical, dynamic Wagnerian sense of awe and anticipation that Ike will feel as he sees the Great Buck for the first time, as well as the capsule vision of Sam Fathers, standing behind young Ike McCaslin, instructing him on how to shoot and how to see and how to feel.

This opening scene emphasizes the fact that Sam Fathers is *behind* the boy, a detail that becomes thematically important in the story because, ultimately, the young boy must learn that all of "the Old People" long dead and departed are *also behind him* and will become aligned with him as he becomes initiated into the mysteries of the wilderness. In fact, the image of Sam standing *behind* young Ike is consistently maintained throughout the story, whether it is the time that the boy shoots his first running rabbit, with Sam standing behind him, or whether it is the time that Sam teaches Ike to put the first load in his first gun on his first hunt, or later on, when Sam Fathers stands behind Ike when he kills his first deer. And finally, in the climactic scene, we see Sam standing behind Ike when Ike sees, for the first time, the Great Buck, the symbol of the spirit of the wilderness.

But Sam is more than just a tutor to the boy; he is also Ike's spiritual guide, and he is the embodiment of all of the noble qualities associated with the pure and uninvolved life that is lived close to nature. Sam is a kind of "priest of nature and of the wilderness," and he must find someone whom he can invest with his heritage. In this way, the spirit of the wilderness, for which Sam stands, will continue to live because it is being invested in someone else, someone who will someday take Sam's place.

The opening of the story, then, shows us Sam as Ike's tutor and spiritual guide, instructing the young neophyte how to kill a deer, and then, symbolically, initiating him and consecrating him into the mysteries of noble hunting by dipping "his [Sam's] hands in the hot smelling blood and [wiping] them back and forth across the boy's face." When the "true hunters" inquire about Ike's performance, Sam vouches for Ike. Faulkner says that Ike had "drawn the first worthy blood which he had been found at last worthy to draw, joining him and the man [Sam] forever, so that the man would continue to live . . . long after the man himself had entered the earth . . . because Sam Fathers had no children." Therefore, Ike is now the young initiate of the wilderness, and the continuance of a noble line of true hunters is insured; Ike will become a future priest of the wilderness.

After establishing Sam Fathers as Ike's tutor and as his spiritual guide, Faulkner gives us information about Sam's background and about Sam's heritage—in particular, Sam's unique combination of blood—Indian, Negro, and white—surging through his veins.

Sam's father (Ikkemotubbe) was a Chickasaw Indian chief, but he was a chief who became chief by using the white man's poison (apparently, arsenic). That is, Ikkemotubbe returned from a visit to New Orleans, where he was called "Du Homme" (shortened to "Doom"), bearing with him a quadroon slave (¾ white, ¼ black) and a basket containing several puppies. Upon arrival, he gave a demonstration: he put a touch of the white powder on the tongue of one of the young puppies, who died immediately. The son of the reigning chief (Mokketubbe, a weak and ineffectual cousin) mysteriously died that night. The next day, Ikkemotubbe gave another demonstration with another puppy, who also died immediately. Mokketubbe abdicated immediately, and Ikkemotubbe became the new chief.

The irony of Ikkemotubbe's "New Orleans'" name now becomes clear: "Du Homme," meaning "the Man" or "the Chief," was corrupted through pronunciation into "Doom," a name particularly apropos to Ikkemotubbe, because it is he who began to sell off the Indian land, land which he had no more right to sell than the white people had the right to buy. He thus created the beginning of the *doom* for the Indian nation, so that by the time of this story, only Sam Fathers and old Jobaker were left in the vicinity.

When Ikkemotubbe's quadroon slave became pregnant, he declared that she was married to one of his black slaves. Her baby was born and was given the Indian name "Sam-Had-Two-Fathers," which was eventually shortened to Sam Fathers. Sam is ½ Indian, ⅜ white, and ⅛ Negro, but in the Southern racial system, Sam's ⅛ Negro blood would mean that Sam was, for all intents and purposes, a "total Negro." But Sam's pride, and knowledge, and heritage allows him to keep to himself and not be readily classified. Faulkner says, "For, although Sam lived among the Negroes, in a cabin among the other cabins in the quarters, and consorted with Negroes (what of consorting with anyone Sam did. . . .) and dressed like them and talked to them, and even went with them to the Negro church now and then, he was still the son of that Chickasaw chief and the Negroes knew it."

Underlying the whole story, then, are the various emphases placed on *blood*. Not only does the warm blood of the deer become the means of Ike's first initiation, but the blood of each character becomes indicative of that character's actions in the story.

The "Old People" in the story have blood which runs cold in their veins; they are correlated with the dead spirits of the past. In addition, Sam Fathers' mixture of Indian, white, and Negro blood gives Sam certain qualities associated with each bloodline. His Indian blood becomes synonymous with the traditions associated with the wilderness and with freedom, but this bloodline has the limitation of being a blood that is isolated. Sam's Negro bloodline is a symbol of the tradition and ritual associated with the Negro race and strengthened by the similar aspects of the Indian blood, but being Negro blood, it is "caged in," thereby caging in Sam's other bloodlines. Sam's white bloodline represents the "civilizing forces," but this is blood which has lost the sense of having a close communion with nature: "When he was born, all his blood on both sides, except the little white part, knew things that had been tamed out of our blood so long ago that we have not only forgotten them, we have to live together in herds to protect ourselves from our own sources . . . himself his own battleground, the scene of his own vanquishment and the mausoleum of his defeat."

Sam, therefore, represents every facet of the freedoms *and* the enslavement of *blood*. It is his Indian and Negro blood which give him his position as a priest of nature, and it is his white blood which gives him his status in the civilized society in which he does "white man's work," mainly carpentry, which is the same type of work which Ike, the young boy in the story, later undertakes in imitation of both Sam and the Ancient Nazarene.

From Sam, Ike learns about the "Old Times, the Old People," and as Sam talks about the past, those "old times would cease to be old times and would become a part of the boy's present . . . the men who walked through them actually walking in breath and air and casting an actual shadow on the earth they had not quitted." This view of the presence of "the Old People," long since dead, prepares the reader for Ike's vision of the Great Buck, the embodiment of the Spirit of the Wilderness which, it is believed, does not cast an actual shadow.

We are also introduced to one of the reasons why Ike, later in "The Bear," relinquishes his hold (or ownership) on the land. In the first place, Ikkemotubbe had no more right to sell the land than

L. Q. C. McCaslin had the right to buy it because *the land belongs to no man* any more than does the air we breathe.

When the only other Indian, the full-blooded Chickasaw Jobaker, who lives as a hermit in the Big Bottom, died, Sam told Cass (Ike's cousin, sixteen years older than Ike) that he wanted to live in the Big Bottom. This happened when Ike was nine and Cass was twenty-five, and it happened at a time when Ike had learned everything that Sam could teach him *in civilization:* "You are ready for the Big Bottom now [ready] for bear and deer . . . ready to become a man." Sam, recognizing that Ike is almost ready to be initiated into the mysteries of the Big Woods and into manhood, symbolically leaves to go into the wilderness himself in order to prepare the way for the young novitiate.

In November, when Ike was ten ("He could count his age in two numbers now"), Ike made his first trip to the Big Bottom, and Sam was waiting for him. After that first year and that first hunt, Ike had learned, among other things, that the Big Woods were not dangerous, and he "brought [back] with him . . . an unforgettable sense of the big woods—not a quality dangerous or particularly inimical, but profound, sentient, gigantic and brooding, amid which he had been permitted to go to and fro at will, unscathed, why he knew not, but dwarfed and, until he had drawn honorable blood worthy of being drawn, alien."

That first time in the big woods, and later, Ike was allotted the poorer stands (the location where one waits for game) because he was only ten, and then eleven, and then twelve, but during these years, waiting at the poorer located stands, Ike learned that invaluable quality of patience, a quality without which any hunter is already doomed, for without patience, a hunt is soon over.

In Part 1, we see Ike's first steps of initiation into the rites of hunting; he learns the proper approach to the wilderness, and he learns which game is to be killed. When he successfully learns these things, he is appropriately baptised with the blood of the first deer that he kills. "Sam Fathers marked his face with the hot blood which he had spilled and he ceased to be a child and became a hunter and a man." This baptism with blood is an acknowledgment that Ike has reached manhood; he has become adept in all the rituals of the wilderness and of the hunt. He has learned the mysteries of the woods and the hunt from Sam—"when to shoot and when not to shoot, when to kill and when not to kill, and better, what to do with it afterwards."

After Ike's baptismal consecration into the mysteries of nature, the woods become less inimical and the wilderness accepts him as a man worthy of the noble qualities to be learned from a life nurtured by nature. In Part 2, we again return to that point when Ike kills his first deer. After reviewing (and retelling) the story of Ike's first initiation, his blood baptism, when Sam "marked him forever one with the wilderness" (note how Faulkner keeps rephrasing, and thus re-emphasizing, Ike's initiation and his consequent unity with the wilderness), we know that Ike is now ready for his *second* initiation.

Ike has been judged worthy enough to draw worthy blood, and Sam can now introduce him into the further mysteries of nature. Even with the first initiation, the boy and the man were, as noted earlier, joined forever "so that the man would continue to live past his seventy years and then eighty years." If Ike had to be taught certain rites in preparation for being initiated into the hunt and into manhood, then his preparation for his second initiation partly began when he listened to the stories of the old times: "those dead and vanished men of another race . . . that the boy knew, gradually to the boy those old times would cease to be old times and would become a part of the boy's present."

We can now look back at Part 1 and see the purpose for the stories about "the Old People." Ike now becomes an integral part of the myths of the past so that the Old Men of the past, those who walked through the same wilderness, are again "actually walking in breath and air and casting an actual shadow on the earth they had not quitted." This introduction into the legends of the past prepares Ike for the spirit of the deer, which casts an actual shadow for Ike, even though it *did not* have substance years ago for his cousin McCaslin.

After reminding the reader of Ike's first initiation, in fact, repeating the same words ("Sam Fathers marked his face with the hot blood . . ."), Part 2 opens at the moment when the annual hunt is over. Camp has been broken, and the hunters are at the edge of the wilderness, when Boon Hogganbeck, notorious for his inability to hit anything with a gun, stops the group and reports that he has seen a buck with at least fourteen points. The men dismount, and under Sam's direction, they spread out over the various trails that the deer might have possibly traversed.

Once again, Ike and Sam occupy a stand at some distance from the other hunters, and during the wait, Ike begins to tremble. He knows, however, that his trembling will cease as soon as he raises his gun to shoot. When they hear a shot—"a single clap of Walter Ewell's rifle which never missed"—Ike is ready to leave, but Sam tells him to wait. At that instant, Ike notices that Sam is standing *behind* him and looking over his head, up toward the ridge. There, Ike sees the Great Buck. It isn't running; it is walking, unhurriedly.

Sam is now ready to present the great spirit of the past to Ike, who will become Sam's successor as the priest of the wilderness. The deer becomes the symbol for the spirit of the wilderness which Sam passes on to Ike, as he acknowledges it to be his ancestor:

> Then it saw them. And still it did not begin to run. It just stopped for an instant, taller than any man, looking at them. . . . It did not even alter its course, not fleeing not even running, just moving with that winged and effortless ease with which deer move, passing within twenty feet of them, its head high and the eye not proud and not haughty but just full and wild and unafraid, and Sam standing beside the boy now, his right arm raised at full length, palm-outward, speaking in that tongue which the boy had learned from listening to him and Jobaker in the blacksmith-shop . . .
>
> "Oleh, Chief," Sam said. "Grandfather."

Ike is ready to be shown the Great Buck. Sam has taught him all the mechanics of the hunt, and, in addition, Ike has killed his first deer. He has become a man. He has been initiated into the rituals of the hunt. He has proved himself worthy of drawing worthy blood. Now, we see him undergoing a second initiation, one which unites him with the spirit of the wilderness after he beheld the Spirit of the Wilderness, represented by the Great Buck.

Part 2 ends with Walter Ewell's report that Boon's huge buck with fourteen points turned out to be just a little yearling. Mysteriously, however, there were other deer tracks, some almost as big as a cow's tracks, as though a *second,* unseen deer were there. Thus, perhaps the Great Buck *could* make tracks, even though it couldn't cast a shadow.

We should also note here the importance of Sam's addressing the Great Buck as "Oleh, Chief . . . Grandfather." Sam associates the Spirit not with his dead father, but with his long dead *grandfather*. To understand this, we must return to Faulkner's theme of the evils that civilization brings to the wilderness. This is first illustrated in the background information that we are given about Sam Fathers' ancestors.

Ikkemotubbe, Sam's father, was the first person to bring the *evils* of civilization into the wilderness. He deserted his native environment and went to New Orleans, where he met the Frenchman who gave him the name of "Du Homme," a foreign, alien name which was corrupted into "Doom." Through his associations with the civilized society, this man actually became the *doom* of the Indian tribe.

From civilization, Doom brought the foreign "Aramis and the quadroon slave woman who was to be Sam's mother," and he also brought the deadly white powder which killed the puppies and Moketubbe's son. This white powder, a product of civilized society, becomes the instrument of doom for the pure relationship that the Indians had with the wilderness, because it was through Ikkemotubbe's *greed* that he began to sell land which did *not* belong to him. Thus, he allowed civilization to begin its encroachment upon the wilderness. Consequently, when Sam acknowledges the spirits of the past, he greets *not* his father, Ikkemotubbe, who represents the evils of civilization encroaching upon the wilderness, but, rather, he greets his *grandfather*, Issetibbeha, who was the last of the Indian chiefs to maintain *a true relationship* with the wilderness.

Part 3 occurs later that night (after midnight), when the hunting party reaches Major de Spain's house, where they will spend the night "since it was still seventeen miles home." Once in the cold bed with his cousin Cass (sixteen years older than Ike), and once the shaking from the cold has stopped, Ike tries to tell his cousin about his experience with the Great Buck, but he feels that Cass doesn't believe him. Yet Cass *does* believe Ike, because he feels strongly that "all the blood hot and strong for living has to be somewhere" because "you always wear out life long before you have exhausted the possibilities of living." In other words, all the experiences of life "must be somewhere; all that could not have been invented and created just to be thrown away." The Old People who once inhabited the earth are still out there, even though "they don't have substance, can't cast a shadow – ." When Ike maintains that he saw the Great Buck, Cass assures him that he believes him; he knows that Ike *did* see the Great Buck because he too once saw the Great Buck. It happened years ago, Cass says, when

"Sam took me in here once after I killed my first deer." (Significantly, the Great Buck did *not* cast a shadow for Cass.)

At the end of the story, Faulkner suggests why Ike was chosen in preference to McCaslin or any of the other "true hunters" to replace Sam. All of them had also been initiated into the spirit of the wilderness, and even though Cass and the other hunters (by implication) had undergone initiation rites similar to Ike's, the spirits of the wilderness seemed like "non-substantial beings" to them. To the other "true hunters," these spirits didn't *really* have "substance, [didn't] cast a shadow."

In contrast, they are real and living entities to Ike and deserve a proper reverence in their own sphere. The implication is that the other hunters are too much a product of civilization to be able to become a pure and unspoiled priest of nature. Only Ike can ultimately replace Sam as Priest of the Wilderness.

THE BEAR

While "The Bear" is one of Faulkner's most celebrated and most praised stories, it presents innumerable and possibly unsolvable problems. For example, while the story consists of five separate parts, there are actually only three large, central concerns in the story.

Parts 1–3 narrate one of the most magnificent hunting stories in all of literature – a story involving the initiation of a young boy into the rituals of hunting and manhood. The long Part 4 is a difficult philosophical discussion between Ike and his cousin Cass, concerning Ike's decision to relinquish and repudiate the family plantation and his inheritance and try to come to terms with the sins of his ancestors. Then Part 5, perhaps the most enigmatic of all the sections, presents Ike's elegiac meditations on the nature of the wilderness and its spiritual values, values which are suddenly intruded upon by the mad, hoarse, strangled threats of Boon Hogganbeck, which end the story on an ambiguous, uneasy note.

Essentially, this is the basic narrative structure of the story, but readers should be forewarned that they will probably find it difficult to discover how Part 4 is related to the other parts of the story. While reading "The Bear," one should remember that Faulkner will intertwine many diverse themes and motifs, but the central concerns of the story will focus on Ike's (or any young boy's) maturation, or coming of age, and his initiation into the rituals of hunting, as well as into the mysteries of the wilderness. In the wilderness, Ike will discover the spiritual values to be discovered from a life lived in close, intimate contact with nature.

At times, Ike's life will transcend the merely physical, and it will become metaphysical and even pantheistic. In the wilderness, he will learn to respect *all* life; he will learn how to live a life worthy enough to be allowed to kill noble game. Part 4, then, correlates the themes of Parts 1–3 and, using Ike's ideas which he learned from the wilderness, Faulkner will apply them to such ethical and humanitarian concerns as (1) the nature of guilt and sin, (2) the nature of incest and miscegenation, (3) the nature of freedom and slavery, (4) of inheritance and repudiation, and (5) of learning to live a true and authentic life.

"The Bear" is a culmination of many themes and ideas that Faulkner has written about elsewhere, and often the same language is repeated to emphasize the same idea – for example, Sam's dipping his hand into the hot, wet blood of the first deer that Ike kills and ritualistically baptising Ike into the wilderness: "Sam stooped and dipped his hands in the hot smoking blood and wiped them back and forth across the boy's face."

In the first three parts of the story, Old Ben the bear will become the symbol of the wilderness, the embodiment of the values associated with a life lived close to primitive nature. The narrative plot-line of these three parts presents an epic-like hunting story; that is, Part 1 recapitulates past events and leads us to Ike's first full view of the great bear. Part 2 depicts the training of Lion, the great mastiff dog, strong enough to bay Old Ben; Lion will be the first to draw blood from the almost mythic-like bear beast. The third part of the story depicts the deaths of Old Ben, Lion, and Sam Fathers, Ike's Indian mentor.

PART 1

The opening line of Part 1 – "There was a man and a dog too this time" – sets the tone, but it quickly looks *backward* in time, as does Part 4, which returns to a much earlier time. But before the flashback, Faulkner establishes a present "time-frame" – when Ike is sixteen years old.

We learn that Ike has hunted yearly in the big wilderness for six years, hearing constantly about, and learning about, the big wilderness – the last land that is still "free." During this time, Ike has constantly heard about Old Ben, the great bear who lives in, and "rules," the wilderness. Old Ben has become a legendary figure, or totem symbol, of monstrous proportions: "The long legend of corn cribs broken down and rifled, of shoats and grown pigs and even calves carried bodily into the woods and devoured . . . dogs mangled and slain and shotguns and even rifle shots delivered at point-blank range, yet with no more effect than so many peas blown through a tube by a child."

Old Ben becomes synonymous with the wilderness which Ike, almost intuitively, knows is rapidly becoming a "doomed wilderness whose edges were being constantly and punily gnawed at by men with plows and axes. . . ." Already in these opening pages of Part 1, some of the novel's central concerns appear: for example, Ike's initiation and participation in the "yearly rendezvous with the bear which they did not even intend to kill," as well as the theme of the disappearance of the wilderness. This latter theme will later be correlated with the ownership of the land and with Ike's ultimate repudiation of the land.

Ike recalls how long he had to wait until he was permitted to enter the wilderness. It happened when he was ten. Faulkner says that Ike "entered his novitiate to the true wilderness with Sam beside him as he had begun his apprenticeship in miniature to manhood." Ike's initiation into the rituals of the hunt becomes synonymous with his entrance into manhood: It seemed to him that at the age of ten he was witnessing his own birth."

Ike vividly remembers the camp experiences – two weeks of sour bread, wild strange meat, harsh sleeping arrangements, and in addition, as the lowest of the plebians, Ike had to take the poorest hunting stands because, as a part of his initiation, he had to learn such things as humility and patience and endurance.

One morning while Ike is ten, he and Sam Fathers, his hunting mentor, are on their stand, waiting for Old Ben, when Sam calls Ike's attention to the strange "moiling yapping" of the dogs, and he says quietly that Old Ben is close by. The old bear has "come to see who's new" this year. He has come, Sam says, "because he's the head bear. He's the man."

Later, back at camp, Sam shows Ike the old bear's claw marks on one of the young, inexperienced hounds. And still later, Sam puts Ike up on the one-eyed wagon mule, the only animal that "did not mind the smell of blood" or the smell of wild animals, or even the smell of Old Ben, because it had known suffering and thus was not frightened of death.

Then Sam mounts another mule, and after three hours of riding, he shows Ike the old bear's footprint – "the print of the living foot." This is Ike's first view of the old bear's footprint, and it will be a long time before he sees Old Ben himself, but from now on, Ike will be able to distinguish Ben's prints, anywhere in the wilderness.

While examining the footprints, ten-year-old Ike announces to Sam that, tomorrow, they will track down Old Ben. Sam, however, contends that "we aint got the dog yet," a statement that anticipates the discovery of Lion in Part 2. Actually, six years will pass before Lion is found. But at the present time, even though Ike is only ten, he *knows* that because the bear has seen *him, he* will *have* to see the *bear:* "*So I will have to see him. . . . I will have to look at him.*"

In June of the next year – *not* during the regular November hunting ritual – Ike tries to track down Old Ben for three days, but he finds nothing. Sam advises Ike that "You aint looked right yet. . . . It's the gun. . . . you will have to choose."

Thus, Ike learns that he will *never* be able to come into contact with Old Ben until he divests himself of all his material ties with civilized society. Before he can carry a gun and confront Old Ben, he must, *first,* confront Old Ben *without* a gun. So Ike, Faulkner says, "left the gun; by his own will and relinquishment"; he left the gun – just as later, in Part 4, he will, "by his own will and relinquishment," give up his inheritance.

Leaving his gun behind, Ike approaches the wooded, dappled milieu of the bear with trepidation, but all the time remembering Sam's admonition: "Be scared. You cant help that. But dont be afraid. Aint nothing in the woods going to hurt you if you dont corner it or it dont smell that you are afraid."

Ike travels farther "into the new and alien country" than ever before. He travels *nine hours,* and then he realizes that Sam didn't tell him everything that he had to relinquish if his quest were to be honorable. It is then that Ike *himself* realizes that in addition to relinquishing the gun, he must also relinquish the watch and the compass – two instruments of civilization. They must also be discarded before Ike can *relinquish himself completely* to the wilderness.

"Then he relinquished completely to it. It was the watch and the compass. He was still tainted. He removed the linked chain of the one and the looped thong of the other from his overalls and hung them on a bush and leaned the stick beside them and entered it."

When Faulkner says that Ike, after removing the tainted objects, "entered it," he means that Ike entered the essence of the wilderness. Ike is already, *physically,* very deep in the wilderness, but here Faulkner means that Ike *spiritually* relinquishes his complete, untainted self to the "wilderness." And ironically, and almost humorously, Ike discovers that he is completely lost.

He has followed all of Sam's instructions, but he cannot find his way back to the watch and compass. It is at this time that Sam as tutor is replaced by Old Ben, who now becomes Ike's mentor.

Ike is sitting on a log, by a little swamp, when he notices Old Ben's footprints; he knows immediately that the old bear is imminent because the tracks are still filling up with water. Ignoring all possibility of danger and without any type of weapon, Ike follows the tracks, and by following them, he is led back to his compass and watch – in other words, back to civilization. Old Ben has become Ike's leader, deliberately leading the lost youth back to his implements of civilization *because* he was brave enough to face the wilderness alone and become one with it. Ike voluntarily relinquished all trappings of civilization, and because of that, Old Ben restored civilization back to Ike.

Furthermore, because of Ike's voluntary relinquishment, Old Ben allows himself to be viewed; "Then he [Ike] saw the bear. It did not emerge, appear: it was just there, immobile, fixed. . . ." Then the bear moves away, slowly. He looks back over one shoulder and is gone. The bear disappears, and Part 1 ends. Ike has experienced his first full view of Old Ben.

The major emphasis in this section has been upon Ike's preparation for the wilderness, his trip into the woods, his relinquishing the "taints" of civilization, his entering the woods, and, finally, his magnificent view of the legendary Old Ben himself.

PART 2

Part 2 of "The Bear" continues Ike's process of learning all about the wilderness, and we see him learning more about it than any of the other hunters. This section also focuses on the courage of the small fyce dog, and the capturing and taming of Lion, the massive dog capable of baying Old Ben. It is here that Lion becomes, as it were, a "character" in this story; in fact, this section opens with the statement that Ike "should have hated and feared Lion." Faulkner says this because, realistically, Lion will become the *instrument of destruction* for Old Ben, and he therefore represents the end of a splendid and noble era associated with the wilderness.

Ike and Sam, however, already recognize the forthcoming destruction of the wilderness and the parts which they must play in the ending of the wilderness. In fact, the final paragraph of this section repeats the opening sentence and clarifies Ike's position: "It was like the last act on a set stage. It was the beginning of the end of something. . . . He would be humble and proud that he had been found worthy to be a part of it. . . ."

By the time that Ike is thirteen, he knows the wilderness as well as anyone; he knows game trails that even Sam Fathers doesn't know about – and now, Ike also knows Old Ben's crooked footprints perfectly. He can find Ben's prints whenever he wishes to, but he knows that no one, including himself, can shoot Old Ben because no dog can hold him at bay.

One June day, Ike brings a young mongrel dog with him to the wilderness; the dog is often called a "fyce" in the South, probably because it is so small and feisty. And this one certainly is – dramatically so in the scene when Ike and Sam ambush Old Ben. The old male bear is so close that the little fyce charges and tries to attack him. At this point, Faulkner says that Ike "flung the gun down and ran. When he overtook and grasped the shrill, frantically pinwheeling little dog, it seemed to him that he was directly under the bear. He could smell it, strong and hot and rank. Sprawling, he looked up where it loomed and towered over him like a thunderclap."

In this scene, Ike observes the young fyce, who possesses the will and the determination and the courage to bay Old Ben, but the dog is physically too small to be effective. He is so small, Faulkner says, that he can't even "see his own shadow." But note that Ike admires the dog's spirit so much that he *drops his gun* in order to recover the dog from under the very paws of Old Ben. In fact, when Ike is asked later how close he was to Old Ben, Ike tells them that he saw a tick under Old Ben's arm.

Significantly, the courage and the spirit of the little fyce and Ike's admiration for the fyce is responsible for Ike's *second* encounter with Old Ben. And it is during this encounter that Sam asks Ike one of the key questions in the story, *Why didn't Ike shoot the bear?* Sam insists: "This time you couldn't have missed." Ike returns the question to Sam: "You had a gun. Why didn't you shoot him!" Neither answers the question because both acknowledge the ritualistic, the mythic, and totemic qualities of the hunt – "it was the pageant-rite of the old bear's furious immortality." The significant words here are "furious immortality." Old Ben has an almost supernatural, raging determination not to be destroyed; seemingly, he will live forever.

Realistically, however, both Ike and Sam know that Old Ben will have to be killed someday, but "it won't be until the last day. When even he don't want it to last any longer." The problem with killing Old Ben is that the "priests of the wilderness," such hunters as Sam and Ike, and the "true hunters," such men as Walter Ewell, Major de Spain, and General Compson, are the only ones who can track the old bear down, and they won't kill him, and the lesser men, who would gladly kill the bear, haven't the ability to track him down.

Returning to the narrative of the story, we learn that there are signs that suggest that Old Ben has "gone wild." Seemingly, he has "broken the rules" by killing a colt, as well as a doe, and "running down a helpless fawn and [killing] it too." Only Sam Fathers knows that these acts are *not* those of Old Ben. Sam knows that these are not Old Ben's techniques because Old Ben kills *only for necessity.* These are *gratuitous killings.*

Sam and Ike examine the tracks of whatever is responsible for the killings, but they say nothing. General Compson and Major de Spain think that the tracks must be those of a panther, or a gigantic wolf. Therefore, they set the hounds to tracking down the unknown beast. But the dogs refuse to follow the scent because they know that the scent is that of another dog.

Using the newly killed colt as bait, Sam is finally able to trap the massive dog – "part mastiff . . . and better than thirty inches at the shoulders and weighing . . . ninety pounds." The dog, Faulkner says, is the color of a gun barrel or a train engine with cold yellow eyes, and thus, from the very beginning, even the color of this animal suggests that it is something mechanical, steady, and impersonal, and Sam knows immediately that here at last is the dog "that's gonter hold Old Ben." While the other hunters totally despair of ever breaking or taming the dog, which they name Lion, Sam maintains that he *doesn't want* Lion tamed.

He then begins the long, deliberate process of starving Lion and then feeding him until he learns obedience. Sam recognizes that Lion possesses all the qualities which he has been searching for in a dog – "a cold and grim indomitable determination." Sam has been looking for a dog who has no concept of fear, who has a disdain for all other animals, including the other hounds. Faulkner says that "Lion neither slept nor ate with the other dogs." He has a fierce pride, a cold and "almost impersonal malignance," and endurance – the will and desire to endure beyond all imaginable limits, and most important, an "indomitable and unbroken spirit."

After Sam trains Lion, it is only fitting that his plebian associate, Boon Hogganbeck, should take care of the dog, and even sleep with it. Ike understands this arrangement immediately because "Sam was the chief, the prince; Boon, the plebian, was his huntsman. Boon should have nursed the dogs."

During the intervening two years, whenever Ike and Sam hunt for Old Ben—technically, the last day of the hunt is always reserved for this annual pageant-ritual—various trappers, farmers, or sharecroppers show up for the hunt. The second year, they jump Old Ben, and Lion holds him at bay, but Boon Hogganbeck, a notoriously bad shot, misses five times, and Old Ben kills a hound and escapes downriver.

Part 2 ends with a third repetition of the line "So he should have hated and feared Lion." Lion symbolizes the end of the annual, traditional ritual hunt. But Ike does *not* hate, nor does he fear, Lion. Faulkner presents Ike as if he were a member of an audience watching the climax of a classical tragedy: "It was like the last act on a set stage. It was the beginning of the end of something. . . ." And, as if we were viewing a classical tragedy, we too both deplore the ending, and yet look forward to it, feeling as Ike does, "humble and proud that he had been found worthy to be a part of it, too, or just to see it too." Part 2 concludes, then, with a sense of Ike's being present in a time when events of a great magnitude are about to occur, and Ike is proud to be a part of these events.

PART 3

This section recounts the last hunt, the hunt which culminates in the deaths of Old Ben, Lion, and Sam Fathers. It is December, a very cold December. The weather has turned bad, and the hunters have to stay in the woods past their regular time; they want to wait for fair weather so that they can take part in Old Ben and Lion's "yearly race." But they have run out of whiskey. At this point, Faulkner takes time out from his narrative and inserts a long digression, one which is interesting in itself, but it contributes little to the story of Old Ben and Lion.

In the digression, Faulkner relates the story of Boon Hogganbeck and Ike's train trip to Memphis – Boon to get more whiskey for the hunters, and Ike to get Boon back to the camp with the whiskey. Clearly, the episode is not central to the main concerns of "The Bear."

With the return of Ike and Boon, the annual, ritualistic hunt for Old Ben begins. Young Ike, who is sixteen, is put up on Katie, the one-eyed mule which is not afraid of either the old male bear or of death.

This recounting of the death of "the bear" is one of Faulkner's finest narrations. In this section, the great dog Lion proves to be the dog who can finally bay Old Ben. All of Lion's training has been designed for this single, climactic moment. That is, Sam recognized early that this mastiff dog was a product of pure strength and determination. Lion showed no allegiance to any person or anything – neither to Sam Fathers nor to Boon. He had a special kind of intelligence, and Sam knew what it was, for in order to perform efficiently and bay Old Ben, the ideal dog would have to be completely devoid of any so-called "human qualities," those qualities which are associated with most other animals, especially with Old Ben himself.

For example, whereas Old Ben "had earned for himself a name, a definite designation like a living man . . . because he's the head bear. He's the man," Lion, in contrast, is described as being like a mechanism which functions *only* as Sam Fathers tells it to function. Lion is a brute force of *civilization* (not a brute force of nature). Lion is like an engine or a train; later on, he will clamp himself onto the throat of Old Ben and hold fast – until destruction is complete. Most of the images used to describe Lion are those of metallic blue or grey, suggesting that he is like an engine or a gun barrel. or like any efficient steel machine.

Even Old Ben seems to recognize that this will be his final battle, the end of the drama in which Ike will, as the others believe, do the actual slaying since he is given the one-eyed, fearless mule. But the hunters are wrong. Ike will, and must, remain a spectator in the final battle. He must remain a part of the audience viewing "the final act." He must watch and do nothing when Lion charges and Old Ben catches "the dog in both arms, almost loverlike. . . ." It is in this scene that Old Ben, while putting up a heroic battle, seemingly embraces death, recognizing that this is the end of a long drama, with the action now complete and the actors spent.

Ironically, it is Boon, and *not Ike* or Sam, who kills the bear. And even though Ike and Sam (and even Old Ben) all recognize the necessity of the bear's death, and even though Ike and Sam set up the scenario in which the bear must die, it would not be in conformity with Faulkner's sense of myth if "the adherents to nature" were to perform the actual slaying.

The god—in this case, Old Ben—must be destroyed by alien hands in order for him to later retain his position as a deity worthy of reverence. Boon's hands are alien hands, and the death that he demands for Old Ben is *not* a noble death. Old Ben is brutally, literally and metaphorically, *ravished* and *raped*. The image of the vice-like jaws of the dog Lion—mechanically clamped onto the bear's throat, with Boon on Old Ben's back, repeatedly stabbing him until he finally manages to reach the heart—forces one to view Old Ben's death in all of its most gruesome and horrifying aspects.

With the death of Old Ben, Lion's and Sam's lives also end. Lion has been trained for only one monumental task, and that task, by its very nature, proves to be suicidal. Once the mastiff dog has clamped its massive jaws around Old Ben's throat, it is as though a mechanical vice had been permanently clasped upon it, and Old Ben has to use his claws to rip out Lion's "belly and guts" to try and loosen him. But Lion never loosens his grip. Sam's training has been effective, and Lion's task is now completed. At sundown, after Old Ben is dead, the large mastiff opens his eyes for one last time "to look at the woods for a moment before closing [them] again." He dies at sundown. Along with Old Ben, Lion is restored to the wilderness in his burial.

Sam, however, was apparently not a witness to the brutal, final part of the drama of Old Ben's death. But the bear and the old Indian/black man were associated for so long with the wilderness that the death of one must necessarily bring about the death of the other. Some time during the scene, we are not sure when, Sam Fathers collapsed, for suddenly Ike saw him "lying motionless on his face in the trampled mud." Apparently having seen enough of the death throes of Old Ben, Sam felt his will to live simply collapsing, or as the doctor says later, "He just quit."

But Sam was not quite dead when he was found, for he pleads with Major de Spain to "Let me go home." And it is then that Boon Hogganbeck, even though he is severely wounded himself, frantically wraps Lion up in his coat, and when he realizes that Sam can't walk, Boon bodily picks the old man up and carries him. Boon remains with

Sam and refuses to let the doctor treat him until Lion and Sam Fathers are treated.

Sam dies two days later, and when the hunters return the following Sunday, they ride past Lion's new grave, and beyond it, they see a "platform of freshly cut saplings bound between four posts and the blanket-wrapped bundle upon the platform." Boon, very drunk and heavy with grief, is confronted by the hunters, and he immediately and loudly asserts that Sam "told us [Boon and Ike] exactly how to do it. And by God you aint going to move him. . . . We did it like he said. . . ."

For some reason, Cass assumes that Sam Fathers asked Boon to kill him and then bury him in the prescribed manner. When Cass persists in trying to find out if Boon did, in fact, kill Sam, Boon is unable to cope, and he falls, plunging against a tree. Only then does Ike intercede between the badgering Cass and the trapped Boon, crying out to his cousin and to the others: "Leave him alone! . . . Goddamn it! Leave him alone!" Thus, the ritual hunt ends, and Ike, while defending Boon, neither affirms nor denies whether or not Boon did actually kill Sam at Sam's request. But the implication is that with the forthcoming demise of the wilderness and with the death of Old Ben, Sam no longer had any sense of belonging to a world that he could call his.

PART 4

Of all of Faulkner's writings, few if any of them have so confused the readers or critics as has Part 4 of "The Bear." Early critics were usually totally perplexed by this section; numerous other, later critics also made many false statements and drew incorrect assumptions about it. Still other critics have found far-out, incredible reasons for its inclusion between Parts 3 and 5, and even when one closely examines it, there seems to be no satisfactory explanation for its inclusion in this long short story.

That is why we return to Faulkner himself for an explanation of this confusing section. First and foremost, according to Faulkner, Part 4 belongs to the entirety of the book *Go Down, Moses* and does not belong, solely and exclusively, to the short story "The Bear."

When Faulkner was a writer-in-residence at the University of Virginia, a student asked him to explain his reason for including Part 4 in "The Bear." He explained that his publisher wanted to publish the story separately, all five parts of it, and because he (the editor) was unable to consult with Faulkner about the publication, he decided to publish "The Bear," all five parts of it, as a very long short story. It was the publisher's decision – not Faulkner's. For Faulkner, Part 4 does not belong exclusively in the short story called "The Bear." "The Bear," according to Faulkner, should consist of only Parts 1, 2, 3, and 5. Part 4 belongs to the entire history of the McCaslin family, as narrated throughout *Go Down, Moses.*

As Faulkner said: "If he [his publisher] had told me he was going to print it separately, I would have said, Take this [part] out, this doesn't belong in this as a short story, it's a part of the novel but not part of the [short] story. . . . The way to read [the short story] is to skip [Part 4] when you come to it."

Thus, Part 4 should be read as a central document concerning the McCaslin, Edmonds, and Beauchamp history and their interrelationships. It is an important statement concerning the various themes found in the entire book of *Go Down, Moses,* and those people who try to relate it directly to the short story, "The Bear," are wasting their time. In order to best understand Faulkner's intentions, we should consider Part 4 as a record of Ike's putting into practice many of the virtues which he learned in "The Old People," as well as during the time-spans of the first three parts of "The Bear" and elsewhere.

Among the concerns of Part 4 are these, principally: (1) Faulkner restates the many virtues which Ike learned from Sam Fathers and from the wilderness, thus relating this section of the story to "The Old People" and to the first three parts of "The Bear." Ike, in fact, later informs his cousin Cass that "Sam Fathers set me free," meaning that the lessons which he learned from Sam allowed him to repudiate his McCaslin inheritance.

(2) The most important concern of the entirety of Part 4 is *why* Ike feels compelled to repudiate his inheritance – a decision that Ike himself does not fully understand. Thus, part of the difficulty of understanding Part 4 is directly related to the fact that Ike's arguments seem *tangled* and *confused* because he himself is trying to seek *rationalizations or justifications* for repudiating the land which he is due to inherit. That is, Ike *feels* and *senses* that his decision is correct, but he can't *logically* defend his decision.

(3) The discussion about Ike's relinquishing his inheritance will

involve Ike's cousin Cass in an evaluation of whether or not the land *can* be owned, and who can own it and how one can claim ownership of a land which God meant to belong to *no one,* in the same way that the air we breathe belongs to no one. These ideas concerning ownership vs. stewardship – that the land was *given* by God to *all men,* that no man has a right to parcel off a bit for himself, and that ownership is contrary to God's intent and will bring a curse upon the land – have already been expressed in "Was" and in "The Old People"; here, in Part 4, they are merely further developed and elaborated on.

(4) Part 4 carries Ike back into the history of the McCaslin family. It is a history that Ike, at age sixteen, started reading about in the ledgers which Uncle Buck (his father) and Uncle Buddy kept long before Ike was born.

(5) The history of the family will reveal to Ike the *sins* which were committed by his grandfather, L. Q. C. McCaslin – sins of such magnitude (*incest,* for example) that Ike's repudiation of his inheritance can be seen as his direct attempt to *atone* for the past actions of his ancestors, from whom he is due to inherit the land.

In addition to the above concerns and directly related to them, Part 4 also contains narratives about (1) Ike's failure (at age eighteen or nineteen) to find Tennie's Jim (a black man), but nonetheless Old McCaslin's grandson, in order to deliver his inheritance to him from his white grandfather, and it also concerns (2) Ike's successful, though disillusioning, tracking down of Fonsiba, Old McCaslin's black granddaughter, in order to give her inheritance to her (or at least leave it with the bank, which will parcel it out to her in three-dollar payments). When Ike finds her, she is so vastly changed that Ike can hardly recognize her as his kinswoman.

In between these concerns is an episode dealing with Uncle Hubert Beauchamp and the fabulous, carefully preserved inheritance which Uncle Hubert has left to Ike – an inheritance which is, ironically, worthless, but its worthlessness is discovered only when Ike is in the midst of renouncing *all* of his McCaslin inheritance, with the realization that "Sam Fathers set me free," a statement which relates most of the themes back to the values which Ike learned in the wilderness.

Part 4 would be easier to read and understand if each of the above concerns were dealt with consistently, chronologically, or logically, and then resolved before moving on to the next concern. However, Faulkner does not present this section coherently. Ike himself frequently shifts ground, and in the midst of one argument, he will offer a long digression about another matter. This absence of ratiocination irritates many critics and readers, and it confuses others who desire a clear and coherent reason for Ike's relinquishment of his inheritance and a logical reason for his repudiation and renunciation of the past actions of his ancestors.

The beginning of Part 4 jumps forward from the time when Ike was in the wilderness, at age sixteen, involved in killing Old Ben, to Ike's twenty-first birthday, the day when he comes into his inheritance and the day when he makes the single most important decision of his life: to relinquish his inheritance. We will discover, in this section, in random, chaotic fashion, what ideas and events of the past have "forced" this decision upon Ike. Seemingly, Ike has no alternative to relinquishing his inheritance, but he cannot, logically, tell anyone, even himself, clearly and coherently, why he *cannot* accept the land bequeathed to him. Throughout this section, Ike seems to be struggling to find some "acceptable reasons," reasons which will be acceptable to other people and to himself in order to explain his relinquishment. Often Ike feels that he is *floundering* in the presence of his cousin (and his father-figure) Cass Edmonds, who is able to counter all of Ike's "feelings" with solid logic.

The scene of the principal argument between Ike and Cass takes place in the commissary, where five years earlier (when Ike was sixteen), he began to read the ancient ledgers, written in cryptic script and kept by his father and his uncle. These are the ledgers which recorded the "manumission in title at least of Carothers McCaslin's slaves." These ledgers will provide the clues to old McCaslin's sins, including the awesome sin of incest.

Part 4 opens with a broad statement concerning the ownership of land—how strong, ruthless, and cynical men bought the land from the Indians (Ikkemotubbe, for instance), who had no right to sell the land since it didn't belong to them to sell—"that not even a fragment of it had been his [Ikkemotubbe's] to relinquish or sell."

To Ike, all the McCaslin land has been gained by *illegal and unethical means,* even though his cousin Cass maintains that it makes no difference *how* the land was originally obtained. The important thing, according to Cass, is that "old Carothers did own it. Bought it, got it, how no matter; kept it, held it, how no matter." In fact, the land has been held in the family long enough for it to be now bequeathed to Ike, the most direct white *male* descendant (according to the law of primogeniture) – that is, Cass was "derived through a woman."

Ike *refuses* to accept Cass' statement that old Carothers "did own" the land. The land, according to Ike, can *never* belong to him (Ike) because it was never his father's or his grandfather's, or even old Ikkemotubbe's to have bequeathed in the first place. Ike says that God created the earth, and He gave man dominion over the animals so that man would hold "suzerainty [feudal-like rights]" over the earth and animals as in the Garden of Eden. Man was to hold the land *only* in the capacity of a feudal-like landlord. He was to hold the land *"in His* [God's] *name."* He was *not* to bequeath it, but to hold it "mutual and intact in the communal anonymity of brotherhood."

In these opening passages, the major theme concerning the ownership of the land is *emphatically* stated by Ike. He will never reverse his opinion. In fact, his opinion will be reinforced by the actions of Uncle Buck (his father) and Uncle Buddy (his uncle), who allowed their slaves to earn their freedom (manumission).

Ike then turns to the lives of his father (Theophilus, or Uncle Buck) and his father's twin brother (Amodeus, or Uncle Buddy), who, upon the death of their father, L. Q. C. McCaslin, immediately moved out of the McCaslin mansion and into a cabin which they built themselves. They then put all the slaves in the big mansion and locked it at night. The slaves could escape through the open, windowless windows, but they were all back inside when the doors were unlocked in the morning.

These two almost identical twin brothers used the ledgers (writing in almost identical handwriting) to record the manumission of the slaves, but we learn that most of them, even after being freed, refused to leave.

From the past history recorded in fragments in the ledgers, we can see that Ike's grandfather (old L. Q. C. McCaslin) acquired *all* of the property, including his slaves, and when he died, Ike's father and uncle were bequeathed the family property (including the slaves). The two twin brothers buried their father and began immediately *dismantling* the estate. First, they repudiated the mansion and allowed the slaves to earn their freedom, a radically liberal and advanced social theory for that time. Ike's *total repudiation* of the land, therefore, is directly related to his father's and his uncle's early attempts to free themselves of the notion of slavery.

As an example of the type of confusing ledger entries which Ike tries to unravel, there is a typical digression in the text (indicated by a parenthesis and lasting over two pages – from near the bottom of page 263 and through page 265 in the Vintage paperback edition). This digression concerns the acquisition of a slave named Percival Brownlee, whom Uncle Buck and Uncle Buddy bought from *"N.B.Forest at Cold Water 3 Mar 1856 $265. dolars"* (before Forrest was a general, while he was still a slave trader). Brownlee, we read, was a *"Bookepper,"* but we discover in another entry that Brownlee couldn't read. There is never any explanation as to why they bought this particular slave; we know that at the same time, they are trying to get rid of their slaves. Percival Brownlee, according to further entries, proved to be so worthless that they tried to give him away, but no one would take him, so they just kept him and renamed him *"Spintrius,"* the Latin (from the Greek) term for a male prostitute.

After this parenthetical, humorous digression, Faulkner prepares the reader for a more serious use of the now-familiar ledgers. Through the ledger entries, we hear of the death of L. Q. C. McCaslin (27 June, 1837), the deaths of two old slaves, Roskus and his wife, Fibby, whose son Thucydus was left a *"10acre peace"* of land in old McCaslin's will. He was also offered, as we later find out, his freedom, but he *"Wants to stay and work it out."*

The above bit of information – that *one particular* slave was left 10 acres of valuable land by old McCaslin – must have immediately aroused Ike's curiosity and suspicions when he read the entry. Why, Ike must have wondered, would *one* slave be singled out to *inherit* a valuable piece of property, especially since it was contrary to all known customs and laws for *any* slave to be permitted to own anything – much less, valuable land.

The answer does not become apparent until we have the complete picture before us; that is, old McCaslin must have arranged for Thucydus to marry Eunice (a black slave) in 1809, because at that time Eunice was pregnant with old McCaslin's child, and by arranging for Eunice to marry Thucydus, and by leaving Thucydus 10 acres of valuable land, old McCaslin was insuring his own future child's welfare by leaving the land to the black slave "father," who would, in turn, leave the land to his heirs. In the total history of the McCaslin family contained in *Go Down, Moses,* this land is the ten acres on which Lucas and Molly (in "The Fire and the Hearth" and elsewhere, such as in Faulkner's *Intruder in the Dust*) are still living.

The ledger entry announcing the death by drowning of Eunice brings forth another suspicious item. Uncle Buddy had written that Eunice *"Drownd herself,"* and two days later, Uncle Buck questions: *"Who in hell ever heard of a niger drownding him self,"* to which Uncle Buddy, the silent but intellectually perceptive twin, writes with total and complete finality: *"Drownd herself."* These, then, are the crucial entries which cause Ike, at sixteen, to take the commissary keys at midnight, when Cass is sleeping, and to return again and again to study the ledgers to try and understand "Why did Uncle Buddy think it strange and unusual that Eunice, a black slave woman, would drown herself?"

Here, in these passages and in spite of Uncle Buck's advanced social views concerning manumission, we can see the typical prejudice of the South—that is, Uncle Buck's incredulity expressed over the impossibility of *any* Negro having feelings profound enough to evoke such an act as suicide.

Thus, this story is thematically tied to "Pantaloon in Black," where the white deputy *cannot fathom* Rider's intense love and grief for his dead wife, Mannie. Likewise, when Uncle Buddy writes *"Drownd herself,"* Uncle Buck responds in the general term which referred at that time to all Negroes: *"drownd him self."* That is, Uncle Buck was not making a specific reference to Eunice, but he is simply revealing a Southern set of mind which categorized all blacks as "him." The typical Southern view—a view that had to exist in order to justify the breaking up of black families in order to sell them to different owners—was that *black slaves were pieces of property,* incapable of such feelings as grief, or love, or remorse, and if they did feel these emotions, it was only transitory.

Faulkner, therefore, presents the colossal irony of Eunice's suicide. Eunice wasn't committing suicide simply because she had had a baby fathered by old McCaslin. She was committing suicide because old McCaslin used Eunice's daughter sexually and violated the most sacred taboo in the world. All civilizations, however primitive, have taboos against incest between parents and children. Old McCaslin had sex with the daughter whom he sired by Eunice, and Eunice, the black mother, found herself in "informal and succinct repudiation of grief and despair." She found that she *could not* live with this knowledge. Thus, she drowned herself.

Ike then discerns from the next entries that Tomasina (Eunice's daughter *not* by Thucydus, as recorded in the ledgers, but by old McCaslin), must have been one-half white. She, in turn, gave birth to "Terrel" (called "Tomey's Turl" in "Was"), who was three-fourths white. Plainly, old McCaslin committed *incest* with his mulatto (half-white, half-black) *daughter*.

Ike is horrified by the thought that his grandfather committed incest with his own daughter, but he cannot escape the *actuality* of the deed. It happened: *"His own daughter His own daughter. No No Not even him."* Knowing this, we can more easily "read between the lines" and realize that when Eunice committed suicide on Christmas Day, 1832, her daughter Tomasina was about three months pregnant with Terrel, who was born the following June, 1833. This explains the $1,000.00 legacy that was left to "the son of an unmarried slave" because that baby (Tomey's Turl in "Was") is old McCaslin's son (and *also his grandson* because of the incest).

Ike then concludes that, for a white man, "leaving money" is easier than *"saying My son to a nigger."* Old McCaslin's attempt to pay off his moral responsibility with money is later brought full circle in "Delta Autumn," when Roth, the great-great-great-grandson of old McCaslin, tries to pay off the great-great-granddaughter of old McCaslin, rather than claim his *illegitimate* son by her.

The next ledger entry records events which were previously narrated in "Was" – that is, the poker game which led to Tennie Beauchamp's marrying Tomey's Turl, and, subsequently, to the birth of their children. The first three children of that union, we learn, did not survive, but the fourth one did. He was James Thucydus (known as "Tennie's Jim"), born in 1864. Then there was a daughter, Sophonsiba (called "Fonsiba"), born in 1869, and then there was the birth of Lucas Quintus Beauchamp (called simply "Lucas"). By now, the black side of the McCaslin descendants had assumed the "Beauchamp" last name.

Ike then remembers that his white father and his white uncle, Buck and Buddy, *increased* old McCaslin's original $1,000.00 legacy to Tomey's Turl to $1,000.00 for *each* of Tomey's Turl's survivors – Tennie's Jim, Fonsiba, and Lucas.

At this point, Ike recalls that when he was eighteen, he traveled in search of Tennie's Jim in order to give him his share – the $1,000.00

inheritance – but he returned home unsuccessful. The $1,000.00 left to Tennie's Jim was left intact. Later, however, Lucas claims both his share *and* his brother Jim's share.

Ike also remembers an incident that occurred one day when Fonsiba was seventeen and Ike was nineteen. On that day, a man who acted and spoke with the authority of a white man appeared out of nowhere, brandishing some "federal papers," supposedly granting him some land in Arkansas. He haughtily announced his intention to marry Fonsiba, and Fonsiba left, but on her twenty-first birthday, when her legacy from old McCaslin came due, Ike traveled to Arkansas to find her.

Ike found Fonsiba in a run-down farm house, with her husband assuming some sort of apocalyptic stance, mouthing idealistic, prophetic words and accomplishing nothing, allowing the land to go fallow. The couple are close to starving, and Fonsiba doesn't even seem aware of Ike's presence, much less the reason why he has come. Ike, therefore, arranges with a banker to pay Fonsiba three dollars a month; he calculates that the $1,000.00 will keep her from starving for at least twenty-eight years.

This episode which focuses on Fonsiba is an important influence on Ike's maturity. He sees Fonsiba, in her run-down farm house, looking like "no one he has ever known," and he feels a sense of alienation and guilt, brought about because of only one reason: because Fonsiba is a *black*, she will *forever* be a *stranger* to him. He tries unsuccessfully to communicate with Fonsiba's husband, who is reading "in the midst of that desolation," decrying that "the whole South is cursed, and all of us who derive from it . . . white and black lie under the curse." *However*, the man rants, the white people's curse is now void because the black people have entered into a new era of freedom, liberty, and equality for all.

Ike, looking about at all the desolation and decay, can only ask, "Freedom from what? From work?" Ike sees that the dream of the black man has been perverted. And it is then that he decides to arrange for his distant kinswoman to receive three dollars a month so that she won't starve.

After the digression concerning Fonsiba, and after the ledger entry announcing the birth of Lucas, and the fact that on his twenty-first birthday, Lucas appeared to Cass and demanded not only his legacy, but *also* Tennie's Jim's legacy, "all of it," Faulkner then returns us to an involved and abstruse discussion between Ike and Cass.

In the commissary, Ike confuses Cass when he continues to try and explain his renunciation of the McCaslin lands. It is simply "something which I have got to do which I dont quite understand myself . . . I dont know why I must do it but I do know I have got to because I have got myself to have to live with for the rest of my life. . . ." Thus, as previously noted, part of the difficulty of Ike's narration in Part 4 is due to the fact that *he does not fully understand* his own reasons for repudiating his inheritance.

Ike and Cass then enter into a discussion of God's intercession into the affairs of men, especially in connection with slavery and the Civil War. Ike believes that God could see within old McCaslin, and there He could envision the men who would be the future Uncle Buck's and Uncle Buddy's – those white men of the South who would someday free their slaves. Ike maintains that God never abandoned the South – that He is still committed to the South because He has done so much for it and for its people. To Ike, God loves the South enough to make sure that it would lose the Civil War because the South *"can learn nothing save through suffering."* Ike sees the South's defeat as part of God's plan to save it.

This discussion leads Ike and his cousin into a discussion of their black Beauchamp relatives, and also to a discussion of the qualities of the black race, in general. When Cass points out the flaws of the blacks, Ike counters with the virtues associated with the Negro people – such superlative virtues as endurance, pity, tolerance, forbearance, fidelity, and love of children – their own or someone else's.

Considering these qualities, Ike is reminded of the many things which he learned from Sam Fathers; he learned humility through suffering, and pride through endurance. To Ike, these are noble values, and these are the very values which he can see within the black race – "honor and pride and pity and justice and courage and love – thus joining his knowledge of the wilderness to his renunciation of his inheritance whose whole edifice intricate and complex [was] founded upon injustice and erected by ruthless rapacity."

Cass attempts to counter Ike's arguments by insisting that the McCaslin property *cannot* belong to the closest descendants to old McCaslin because the *closest* descendants *are black*. And, moreover, they have chosen the name of "Beauchamp" instead of "McCaslin."

And, Cass says, he himself comes from the female line; only Ike, the *true, white* grandson *from the male line* should inherit the property. Ike is "the third generation, and the male, the eldest, the direct and the sole and white and still McCaslin even, father to son to son." Therefore, Cass says, *logically,* the inheritance should be Ike's. And even if the land once belonged to Sam Fathers (old Ikkemotubbe's son), Ike is Sam Fathers' *spiritual inheritor* of all that Sam owned and possessed. To Cass, Ike seems twice blessed to be chosen to receive the McCaslin lands.

Ike can only counter this argument by saying that it was "Sam Fathers [who] set me free." The argument closes as Ike foresees a future in which he will move into town, carrying with him his new carpenter's tools and General Compson's silver mounted hunting horn (which Ike, in "Delta Autumn" will pass on to Roth's illegitimate son, who is also Ike's first cousin, thrice removed) and in addition to the silver hunting horn, a "bright tin coffee pot," Ike's sole material inheritance from the Beauchamps.

Suddenly, there is apparently a complete shift in Faulkner's focus. It is as though Ike visualizes the coffee pot and suddenly recalls its history as his sole inheritance from his Uncle Hubert Beauchamp. Initially, Ike's inheritance from Uncle Hubert was to be a silver chalice (or cup), filled with gold pieces; it was wrapped in burlap and sealed in wax, to be opened on Ike's twenty-first birthday.

Through the years, however, when Hubert's gambling debts would mount up, the gold pieces were borrowed back and replaced by Uncle Hubert's IOU's. And finally all of the gold pieces were gone, and there was nothing to use as collateral but the silver chalice itself. But eventually it was lost in a poker game and replaced by a "bright tin coffee pot." And this is all that Ike received as a Beauchamp "legacy."

Ironically, at the very moment when Ike is formally repudiating his vast McCaslin inheritance, he discovers that his fabulous, legendary Beauchamp inheritance, dreamed of so often during his youth, is worthless.

This entire digression is a comment on the nature of inheritances, particularly significant in this case because it comes at the exact time when Ike is *trying to justify his renunciation* of his *very valuable* McCaslin inheritance.

After Ike repudiates the McCaslin lands, both Major de Spain and

General Compson offer him a place to stay, even though General Compson's reason for doing so is partly to discover *why* Ike gave up his inheritance: "It looks like you just quit, but I have watched you in the woods too much and I dont believe you just quit."

Ike does accept some money from his cousin Cass "as a loan," and he buys his carpenter tools, not merely in "static and hopeful emulation of the Nazarene . . . but . . . because if the Nazarene had found carpentering good for the life and ends He had assumed and elected to serve, it would be all right too for Isaac McCaslin." Thus, Ike chooses to lead a very simple, passive life, hoping to avoid harm, living a quiet exemplary life, as Sam Fathers lived, close to the essentials of life. And by assuming a life void of materialist things and of all property, Ike thereby emulates both Sam Fathers *and* the Ancient Nazarene.

But unlike the Ancient Nazarene, who adhered to both poverty and chastity, Isaac marries a woman, an only child, whose father told her about the McCaslin plantation. Ironically, this woman loved Ike and married him, but she was obsessed with a dream of being rich, of being the mistress of a grand mansion and reigning over a vast plantation.

Part 4 closes with a very moving and powerful temptation scene. Ike loves his wife deeply, and because of this love, he desires to "see her naked because he loves her." And yet, because of his wife's extreme modesty, she has never allowed Ike to have even a glimpse of her naked body. Now, however, when he wants to see her naked body, she discovers that he is building them *a bungalow in town.* She wants nothing less than a mansion and a plantation; nothing less will do. So she locks the door to their rented room, ignores the calls of the landlady, throws away her modesty, strips completely naked, and invites Ike to "take off your clothes." Using the eternal temptation of the naked woman, she tries to exort a promise from Ike that he *will repossess the plantation.*

Part 4 ends with her pleading and with Ike's saying, over and over, "No, I tell you. I wont. I cant. Never." Ike realizes that *"She was born lost. We were all born lost."*

As we will discover later (in "Delta Autumn"), Ike's wife will never again allow Ike in her bed. Ike saw her naked only because she wanted to seduce him and make him promise to reclaim the McCaslin mansion and its plantation.

Ike not only renounced his inheritance on that night, but he real-

ized that because he wouldn't repossess the plantation, he was renouncing all his heirs that he hoped for. His wife will give him no
children unless he promises her a mansion and a plantation.

As a result, Ike becomes "Uncle Ike" to half the county and father
to none. In his wife, Ike realized that few human beings are really
capable of renouncing material wealth in order to live, as Sam Fathers
did, close to nature and free of materialistic matters. Ike now fully
realizes that Sam Fathers did indeed "set me free" by showing him
that the path to true freedom, as the Ancient Nazarene preached,
means a renunciation of material possessions.

In general, then, Part 4 has shown us how Ike utilized the values
which he learned in the wilderness – patience, humility, love, endurance, and justice – in order to evaluate his own relation to his inheritance, to his ownership of land, and to his relationship with other
people, both black and white, and to his own sense of freedom from
any type of enslavement. Ultimately, Ike follows Thoreau's dictum:
a man is wealthy only in proportion to those things which he can
afford to do without.

PART 5

Part 5 of "The Bear" returns us to Ike's eighteenth year, three years
before his decision to renounce, absolutely, his inheritance; thus, we
are also back to a time two years after the deaths of Lion, Old Ben,
and Sam Fathers. During these two years, Major de Spain has sold
large portions of the wilderness to a lumber company. The annual
hunting parties (both the double birthday celebration in June and the
ritual hunt in November) have been disbanded, and, in addition, a
narrow gauge railroad has been built into the wilderness. Slowly and
imperceptibly, the wilderness is giving away to "progress."

The second fall, Ike visits Major de Spain to get permission (a mere
courtesy) to hunt on the remaining land and to arrange a rendezvous
with Boon Hogganbeck here. De Spain makes the arrangements and
sends provisions and old Ash to cook for them.

Part 5 begins with a sense that the great events of the past – those
events which Ike felt proud to have been worthy to have been a part
of – are now rapidly disappearing, and instead of the great hunts of
the past, there is only Boon Hogganbeck (whose gun never hits
anything), himself, and old Ash.

Ike will continue to go on an annual hunt (see "Delta Autumn") even when he is well into his seventies, but it will never again be the same as it was when Sam Fathers was alive, and after this time, he will *never again return* to this particular place, the scene of Sam's and Lion's and Old Ben's graves.

After a delightful digression about a young bear which was frightened by a locomotive, climbed a tree, and remained there for thirty-six hours, Faulkner tells us that Ike arrived on the little log-train, and he found Ash waiting for him.

Ash tells Ike that he is to meet Boon at "the Gum Tree . . . a single big sweet-gum just outside the woods, in an old clearing," where one could surprise and trap a dozen squirrels because there was no other tree they could leap to. With this information, Faulkner prepares us for our final encounter with Boon, sitting under this tree, filled with trapped and frantic squirrels. Likewise, when old Ash warns Ike to watch his feet, "They're [snakes] crawling," Faulkner is anticipating Ike's encounter with the great rattlesnake.

All alone, on his way to meet Boon, Ike recalls some of the old times, old times like the time when Ike killed his first buck, and "Sam marked his face with its hot blood," a statement which was repeated often in "The Old People," throughout the first three parts of "The Bear," and which will again be recalled in "Delta Autumn," thus unifying these stories by this central motif.

This digression also focuses on the time when old Ash wanted to use his carefully-preserved-over-the-years shells to hunt a bear. It is a digression that is used to recall insignificant but previous memories of the past and to indicate Ike's frame of mind as he approaches the graves of Old Ben and Sam Fathers. Ike easily finds the grave, simply by utilizing all of his knowledge about the wilderness that he had originally learned from Sam Fathers. He arrives at the plot which Major de Spain held back and reserved from the sale to the lumber company. It is clearly set off by four concrete markers. Ike is immediately caught up in the mystery of nature, and in the notion of death, here in this "place where dissolution itself was a seething turmoil of ejaculation tumescence conception and birth, and death did not even exist." After two years, there was no clear trace of the graves, but Ike, using his immense knowledge of the wilderness, is able to find the exact spot where "Old Ben's dried mutilated paw" was buried in a tin box, resting above Lion's bones.

As Ike wanders about the burial ground, he feels spiritually connected to Sam Fathers (and also, by analogy, to all of the old people
from "The Old People") as he thinks that Sam *"probably knew I was
in the woods this morning long before I got here."*

After paying homage to Sam Fathers by leaving a twist of tobacco,
a new bandana handkerchief, and some peppermint candy, Ike im-
merses himself in the still mysteries of the wilderness – a wilderness
"which, breathing and hiding and immobile, watched him . . . from
beyond every twig and leaf until . . . quitting the knoll which was
no abode of the dead because there was no death, not Lion and not
Sam; not held fast in earth but free in earth and not in earth but of
earth, myriad yet undiffused of every myriad part, leaf and twig and
particle. . . ." Ike, in this moving and elegaic paean to nature, correlates all of the forces of the wilderness against which man must con-
tend. He realizes that man can become one with the wilderness only
by yielding to its mystical powers, by loving and respecting it, seeing
in nature, as Wordsworth saw, the power to love and to chastise.

As Ike is feeling at one with the wilderness, he suddenly encoun-
ters a huge, six-foot rattlesnake, "the old one," which moves away,
but as it does, it carries with it something of the Garden of Eden ("the
ancient and accursed about the earth"). It carries itself erect, and Ike
salutes it: "'Chief,' he said: 'Grandfather,'" using the same salutation
that Sam Fathers used, six years ago, when he saluted the Great Buck
which cast no shadow (at the end of "The Old People"). And just as
the Great Buck represented the spirit of the unseen mysteries of the
wilderness, here Ike salutes the snake, using the same gesture ("one
hand raised") that Sam Fathers used six years ago, thus correlating
the mystical qualities of the wilderness in both stories.

Ike's pantheistic communion with the wilderness is suddenly and
harshly interrupted by metallic, hammering sounds. Approaching the
sounds, he sees Boon Hogganbeck sitting under the solitary gum tree,
which seems to be alive with frantic trapped squirrels. Boon has
dismembered his gun and, in a frenzy, he is hammering the barrel
against the breech (we assume that he is trying to dislodge a jammed
shell). Without even looking up to see who is approaching, Boon
screams out: "Get out of here! Dont touch them! Dont touch a one
of them! They're mine!"

The ending is troublesome for many readers. Some readers object
to it simply because Ike's peaceful and calm communion with nature

is so harshly intruded upon by this clanging noise. Others object to the ending because Boon's defiant assertion to his friend Ike seems so uncharacteristic.

Yet, Boon's cry presents the only alternative to Ike's response to the destruction of the wilderness. From the values which Ike received from the wilderness, he will be able to renounce not only his own inheritance, but he will be able to renounce all concepts of ownership and will be able to establish a meaningful life for himself. Confronted with the destruction of the wilderness by civilization, Boon sets up boundaries of "thine" and "mine," and having witnessed the encroaching destruction of his world, he can only cry out in pathetic and frantic desperation that this small part of the remaining wilderness — the single tree filled with frenzied squirrels — is his: "They're mine!"

DELTA AUTUMN

In terms of Faulkner's total writings about the McCaslins, especially in "The Old People" and in "The Bear," one of the important concerns of this story is *how Ike conducted his life during the intervening years* between his reading the McCaslin history in the commissary ledgers (in "The Bear") – when he rejected, or repudiated, his inheritance – and now, in the present, some fifty-two years later. Likewise, readers and critics are interested to find out how Ike ("Uncle Ike" to over half the county) used the knowledge he gained from his initiation into the wilderness. That is, they wonder if he has contributed to society, or if he has benefited humanity in some way.

It is, therefore, important to note that the main action of this story takes place, once again, in the wilderness. It was over fifty years ago in the wilderness that Ike learned about honor and courage and truth and compassion – and love.

Significantly in this story, which focuses on an older Ike, Ike does *not* respond here with love or pity or compassion to a woman who is a distant kinsman of his. Nor does he respond positively to the child which she carries in her arms, even though the child was sired by Ike's distant kinsman, Roth. What Faulkner sets up is a dramatic climax of immense social and sexual ramifications.

Slowly, Ike realizes that the woman standing before him carries his bloodline and also Roth's bloodline, but more important even, she is a black woman who passes for white. Roth, then, not only committed miscegenation (they lived as man and wife for six weeks in New Mexico), but as though the old family curse of incest is reappearing, he has also fornicated with his cousin and rejected his part-black son.

Critics have not been kind to Ike's shocked reaction, when he discovers that the woman before him is the granddaughter of Tennie's Jim (James Beauchamp, the grandson of old Carothers McCaslin, who is also Ike's grandfather. Tennie's Jim, remember, is the black man whom Ike tried to trace down and give him his McCaslin inheritance – see Part 4 of "The Bear").

Ike's stunned reaction to the woman, "You're a nigger," seems to be totally uncharacteristic of the Ike who *repudiated* his background and his inheritance because of (1) old Carothers McCaslin's callous treatment of his slaves and (2) because of old Carothers McCaslin's incestuous relationship with this very woman's *great-great-grandmother,* Tomasina. Ike remembers all too well the horror he felt when he discovered in the ledgers that his grandfather had a Negro mistress and that he had sex with his own daughter by that Negro mistress. Yet now, years later, here is the great-great-granddaughter of that morally and legally sinful union, standing before him.

Ike finds it impossible to fathom. His response to this seemingly impossible coincidence is: *"maybe in a thousand or two thousand years in America . . . But not now! Not now!"* This outcry seems uncharacteristic of the idealistic, humble, and loving Ike whom we knew over fifty years ago. And yet, to judge Ike fairly, we should consider the social circumstances of that time.

When the story opens, as noted above, fifty-two years have elapsed since we last heard of Isaac McCaslin (now "Uncle Ike" to most of the people who know him), in the fourth section of "The Bear," when Ike was twenty-one. Uncle Ike is now seventy-three and is still continuing the annual hunting ritual, renewed every fall, even though "he no longer told anyone how near eighty he actually was because he knew as well as they did that he no longer had any business making such expeditions."

Now, however, there is a tremendous difference between the two ritual hunts: then, fifty-two years ago, the hunters were the old "true hunters" – Major de Spain, Walter Ewell, General Compson, and Roth's grandfather, Cass – riding in a wagon pulled by mules. They set out to hunt all kinds of game, including bear: "There had been bear then. A man shot a doe or a fawn as quickly as he did a buck . . . but that time was gone now."

Now, the hunters have to drive over two hundred miles on concrete highways in order to reach the rapidly disappearing wilderness. And instead of the slow moving wagon, they now speed along the highways with reckless abandon.

But the hunts have remained. There have been sixty-three annual hunts since Ike's first hunt, at the age of ten. At that time, Ike was the initiate, the recipient of old Sam Fathers' knowledge of the wilderness. Now, Ike himself is, and has been, the teacher, the tutor, and the mentor. He has taught the "sons of his old companions how to distinguish between the prints left by a buck or a doe." In other words, for years, Ike has served the same function that Sam Fathers served for Ike in "The Old People" and in "The Bear."

The first significant and jarring event in the story occurs when one of the hunters, Ike's great nephew Roth Edmonds, slams on the brakes of the car, throwing Uncle Ike suddenly forward toward the dash. (Roth is the present owner of the plantation *which Ike rejected* and on which Lucas Beauchamp, the woman's great uncle, hunted buried treasure in "The Fire and the Hearth"). But it is not until almost the very end of the story that we learn the reason for Roth's sudden braking. Roth suddenly saw his mistress, the mother of his child, standing alongside the road, holding her and Roth's infant child in her arms.

At this point, another hunter in the car, Will Legate, begins teasing and badgering Roth. Earlier Roth had announced that he would *not* join the annual hunt this year. Legate teases Roth, using deer hunting terminology and suggesting that Roth is not hunting "bucks" – that is, male deer – instead, Legate says, Roth has "a doe in here . . . one that walks on two legs . . . pretty light colored, too."

Had Ike been listening closely and had he been intellectually alert and astute, he might have realized that Legate, in using the word "doe," was referring to a female with whom Roth was having an affair. Moreover, hunting does is *illegal* in this day and age. Even more important, however, is the term "light colored," which Legate uses to goad Roth for having an illegal affair with a Negro woman, even though she is light-colored enough to pass for white.

But Ike is too involved in his own thoughts to catch the implications of Legate's figurative joshing. Even when Legate makes such obscene racial puns as Roth's going "coon-hunting," Ike is deaf to the implication. But Roth is not. He knows what Legate is doing. Legate's emphasis on Roth's "doe hunting" also suggests a lack of firm morals on Roth's part since anyone who would hunt does might well act dishonorably toward his black mistress and their mutual child. With bitter irony, Faulkner concludes this story with the announcement that Roth has illegally killed a real doe, a forbidden act now that the wilderness has almost disappeared.

Along with this conversation, and in addition to Ike's remembering how, on the last hunt, Roth had gone to town for supplies and had stayed over and had come back a drastically different and changed man, we also learn that Roth continued his affair with his distant black kinswoman, meeting her in New Mexico and living with her during the month of January because no one in New Mexico would notice or be concerned with her trace of black blood. Furthermore, we must assume that the baby was conceived in January and was born in October since it is only an infant in November, at the time of this story.

Uncle Ike, however, is also oblivious to these implications. Seemingly, at this point, he is even blind to Roth's bitter, negative attitude. It is as though Ike's age has blurred his vision to the obvious. Instead, Ike is consumed with considering the vast differences between the wilderness today – and when he first began to hunt.

When Ike first began to hunt, the wilderness was only thirty miles away; now it is over two hundred miles away. For Ike, the old times were better times. Men were more self-reliant then. The "true hunters" in the old days, such men as Major de Spain and General Compson – long since dead – have been replaced by a somewhat negative, quarrelsome, cynical generation of young men who violate the law by killing does and then covering up with lies for one another.

The fraternity and the fellowship of the old hunters has been replaced by cynical teasing and testing. And the old wilderness has been replaced by super highways and steel railroads. Yet, not all is gone, entirely. After the two-hundred-mile ride, they still have to use boats and pitch tents (the old cabins in the woods have long since been torn down), and today they sleep, if not on the ground, on portable cots. There is still an element of "roughing it," but it is only a very thin trickle of the strong feeling that once surged through the blood of the old and the "true hunters."

When they finally reach the campsite, there is only two hours of daylight left, and so Ike sends two of the Negroes to cut firewood, and he tells them to cook up the "town food" so that there won't be "a piece of town meat in camp after breakfast tomorrow." This is in keeping with his past experiences, when hunters ate only what they killed – bear, deer, turkey, or coon.

But times are different now, as Legate points out, because in the old days, he says, "they shot does too . . . now, we ain't got but one doe hunter." Once again, Legate's searing allusion does *not* register with Ike, but the remark *does* prefigure the end of the story, when Roth actually will kill a doe.

Roth cynically believes that Ike's feelings about the past are too simple and too sentimental; sarcastically, he urges Ike to say that not only were the "old times better," but that *then*, "better men hunted." Ike does not take the bait. He simply offers Roth the true humanitarian's concept: "There are good men everywhere, at all times. Most men are [good] . . . because most men are a little better than their circumstances give them a chance to be."

In other words, Ike still believes that, *given the chance*, man is essentially good, and *given the circumstances*, man can rise to the occasion and prove himself noble, or in Faulkner's later words, "Man shall not only endure, but he shall prevail."

Roth's response to Ike's view of man is sardonically stated in an insult to Ike and in an insult to Ike's view of humanity: "So you have lived almost eighty years . . . and that's what you finally learned about the other *animals* you lived among. I suppose the question to ask you is, *where have you been all the time you were dead?*" [my italics].

Roth's crude and obscene remark about Ike's being "dead" startles and shocks the others. But these derisive and cynical views are consistent with Roth's later trying to use "blood money" to pay off his obligations to his mistress (and his child), and still later, Roth's illegally killing a doe and then frantically trying to conceal it. But Uncle Ike calmly *reasserts* his belief that "God created man and . . . the world for him to live in" – that is, God created the earth as though He Himself desired to live on it.

After the hunters retire, Ike lies awake on his cot and reminisces about the old times. In this interlude, many of the ideas and themes already explored in the other stories are restated, so that even without a knowledge of the previous stories, we are given enough information to establish or re-establish the basic themes of each story.

Ike recalls his relationship with old Sam Fathers, who initiated him into all the rituals of hunting and baptised him into the spirit of the wilderness. Old Sam Fathers was with him when he killed his first buck, and he was with Ike when Ike bled the buck with Sam's knife, and it was at that time that "Sam dipped his hands into the hot blood and marked his face forever." Ike remembers his oath at his initiation: *"I slew you; my bearing must not shame your quitting life. My conduct forever onward must become your death."* This thought reminds Ike of his repudiation, at twenty-one, of his inheritance.

Ike's repudiation of the McCaslin lands is directly related with the failure of his marriage and with *his wife's repudiation of him* because he *refused to reclaim* his land and his inheritance. Thus, he lost his wife. But not before she tempted him, tempted him as the eternal seductress, when she exposed herself: "the first and last time he ever saw her naked body." But Ike refused to reclaim the *tainted land.* He didn't want it for himself, and most of all, he didn't want it for the son he hoped to have. But Ike lost not only his wife, but he also lost the son he hoped for. After she left Ike, because she loved possessions more than she loved him, Ike *lost all hope* of ever having a son. The irony is overwhelming. Night after night, before he was even twenty-one, he agonized over how best to deal with his grandfather's tainted land. Finally, he rejected it, even though it was worth a fortune. As a result, he lost all hope of ever having a son.

Finally, Ike sleeps. When he is awakened, it is by Roth, giving Ike an envelope and telling him that he is to give it to someone who "might come" to their camp. If that person comes, Roth says, Ike is to give that person the envelope and tell that person "No." Ike is not happy to be placed in such a position, and so he asks Roth directly, "What did you promise her that you haven't the courage to face her and retract?" Ike finds Roth totally reprehensible, and he confronts his kinsman with his cowardice. Roth cannot face the confrontation, however, and leaves.

It is only a short time before a young woman arrives, carrying a small child in her arms. Immediately, Ike demands to know if the child is Roth's and the woman confirms it. Ike tries to give her the envelope and dismiss her, saying, "Here. Take it. Take it." But she simply stares at him and says, "You're Uncle Isaac."

Because of the young woman's search, or "hunt," for Roth, we are carried back to "Was," the first story in this volume, the story that introduced the "ritual of the hunt." During that "hunt," Uncle Buck and Cass were out hunting for *their* Negro kinsman, Tomey's Turl. Today, however, this young woman stands before Ike and tells him about that day so long ago in the past.

That day, she says, "Your [Ike's] cousin McCaslin was there . . . when your father and Uncle Buddy won Tennie from Mr. Beauchamp for the one that had no name but Terrel so you called him Tomey's Terrel, to marry. But after that it got to be Edmonds." Here, before Ike (even though he does not recognize her yet), is Tomey's Turl's great-granddaughter, another descendant, just like Ike, of old Carothers McCaslin. And she is trying to hunt down a man who is also a descen-

dant of old Carothers McCaslin, and moreover, one who has no more
concept of honor and ethics than did the old progenitor of the clan.

Ike does not *yet* recognize her – even though the woman calls him
Uncle Ike. But Ike *will soon recognize her,* and he will have to once
again confront the old problem which he confronted in the ledgers –
that is, the problem of the white man's "prerogative" to impregnate a
Negro kinsman, and then to "buy" immunity from the act with money.

Old Carothers McCaslin left an inheritance to the blacks whom
he sinned against, and now, Roth leaves money in an envelope for
his black mistress and their child. Roth thinks that he can *pay her
off.* Seemingly, fate is punishing Roth for his attitude by arranging,
in the most shocking way imaginable, for him to try and "pay off"
his own fourth cousin, a black woman.

When Ike gives the woman Roth's money, she dumps it onto the
bed and says, "That's just money." And suddenly Ike is aware that
she has *not* come to extort money from Roth. But, if not for money,
why *has* she come? He continues questioning her about her motives
for coming to the camp, but his questions elicit no answers. Instead,
she tells Ike the story of her affair with Roth in New Mexico, where
she lived with him for six weeks, "where I could at least sleep in the
same apartment, where I cooked for him and looked after his clothes."
This last statement should have been yet another clue to let Ike know
that the woman is part Negro, but again, Ike doesn't catch on.

The woman continues to explain to Ike that she and Roth agreed
to separate after their six-week affair in New Mexico, and she reveals
that Roth has already sent money for the birth of the baby. Ike continues to insist on knowing why she has come, and she continues to
digress, this time telling Ike that Roth has been spoiled – not only by
Uncle Lucas and Aunt Mollie, but mostly by Ike himself because he
gave the McCaslin lands to Roth's grandfather, lands "which didn't
belong to him, not even half of it by will or even law." She says that
Roth has never faced the problem of "growing up." She maintains that
she could have made him into a man, and that she is here now to
see if it still might be possible. But all that has changed. Now that
she has seen the envelope with the money, she knows that it is too
late for Roth to change and, thereby, "save himself."

When Ike asks her if she has any relatives at all, the woman men-
tions an aunt who has a big family, a woman who takes in washing.
And it is now, after Ike has missed clue after clue as to the woman's

genetic heritage, that it finally dawns on Ike: "taking in washing" is done only by Negroes.

Now Ike "understood what it was she had brought into the tent with her, what old Isham had already told him by sending the youth to bring her in to him – the pale lips, the skin pallid and dead-looking yet not ill, the dark and tragic and foreknowing eyes. *Maybe in a thousand or two thousand years in America,* he thought. *But not now! Not now!* He cried out loud, in a voice of amazement, pity, and outrage: 'You're a nigger!'"

His discovery that the woman is part Negro is quickly followed by the revelation that (1) she is also a distant kinswoman, that (2) both she and Roth are direct descendants of old Lucius Quintus Carothers McCaslin, and that (3) both of them are fourth cousins.

Immediately upon hearing that the woman is the granddaughter of James Beauchamp, old Carothers' grandson, Ike wants to know if Roth knew about the distant blood relationship. She tells him no. Ike is still stunned, however. Roth and this woman have re-enacted an old drama, a parallel of the original, incestuous act which caused Ike, over fifty years ago, *to repudiate his inheritance.* He was *not* able to remove the curse that lay on the tainted McCaslin lands, after all.

He becomes emotionally distraught and cries out in a "thin . . . and grieving voice: 'Get out of here! I can do nothing for you! Can't nobody do nothing for you!'" Then, just as she is ready to go, Ike calls to her and tells her to take the money on the cot. She says that she doesn't need it. But Ike, having tried years ago *to buy his own immunity from sin* by repudiating a great wealth, *demands* that she take the tainted money. He frantically implores her: "Take it out of my tent."

She takes the money, and Ike touches her for a second, feeling "the strong old blood." He learns that the baby is a boy, and so he makes a token gesture to his and Roth's new, young kinsman: he gives the boy the old silver hunting horn which once belonged to old General Compson, a symbolic gift – in silent and secret recognition of the kinship which can never be publicly acknowledged.

Ike then advises the woman to go North and marry. He tells her to marry "a man of your own race. . . . Marry a black man. You are young, handsome, almost white. . . . Then you will forget all this, forget it ever happened, that he ever existed." Clearly, Ike, a product of his Southern society, the Civil War, and the burning issue of racial discrimination, cannot accept *any type* of miscegenation, even when the amount of black blood is miniscule, and even when the woman is predominantly white. In fact, the woman can pass for white. But because the woman has even *some* black blood in her, the old curse of slavery, of black/white relationships overcomes any abstract and perhaps noble feelings that Ike might have entertained – had she been white.

Ultimately, even Ike, raised in the wilderness to value truth and compassion and love, tries to "buy her off," in the very same way that old Carothers tried "to buy off" his own black children and grandchildren. And Ike fails to fathom that the woman came for love – not for money. And this is why she asks Ike, finally: "Old man . . . have you lived so long and forgotten so much that you dont remember anything you ever knew or felt or even heard about love?" Then she leaves him.

She will never know the devastating effect of her question. Ike, who is "uncle" to half the county, sacrificed *all* his chances of patrimony (fatherhood), and he will *never* have the son he yearned for, the son he hoped to save from owning the "tainted" McCaslin lands. As Faulkner reminds us, the woods and the wilderness are Ike's *only love* – his only wife and mistress now, the only love he has, and now they are disappearing, and this woman has doubted Ike's ability to love – at the very moment when he, after having lost a wife and an unborn son, is in the midst of the very wilderness he loves so deeply, and just as he realizes how transient even the wilderness is.

Ike's summing-up is confirmed by the brief ending of the story, when Will Legate frantically comes in and searches for a knife, apparently to skin and dress a deer before it is discovered by a game warden, and thus *cover up* for the illegal act of killing a doe. Ike's realization that Roth has illegally killed a doe (illegal, according to the present laws of the wilderness) brings the story to an end, with the metaphor of "doe killing" being applied to both Roth's present actions and his rejection of the woman and his own child. In both shameful acts, Roth has rejected ethical, humanitarian behavior and has substituted illegal and unethical behavior.

In the final analysis, as we measure Ike's actions in this story, we must take into account the times and the society that Ike lived in. We cannot condemn so broadly, like the woman who came to the camp, who in her bitterness condemned not only Uncle Lucas and Aunt Mollie for spoiling Roth, but Ike also, for keeping Roth from becoming a man capable of love and responsibility. We must view Ike's renunciation of the land as an act to be judged by his intention: Ike wanted to atone for the sins of his grandfather, and giving up the valuable legacy of land seemed to be the best possible act of sacrifice and expiation.

Ultimately, it is not so much what Ike *didn't do* or what he *did do* that concerns us. That is, the greatness of Isaac's life doesn't lie in the active deeds that many critics expect of him, but, instead, Ike's greatness lies in the quiet, exemplary life which he led – a life of partial asceticism and a great deal of sacrifice, a life of doing no harm and no evil, of trying to find only the best in other people. In the words of a Southern critic, Andrew Lytle, Faulkner created a "believable individual, of a certain heritage, in a certain time and place, acting among individuals who perform out of the mores of a society." Thus, if Isaac is a disappointment to those critics who expect him to present *the ideal solution* to the race problem, those critics should remember the exact nature of the society of the nineteenth century which existed in the South while Ike was growing up.

In summary, Ike possesses qualities that make him one of Faulkner's most intriguing characters. While being only a common carpenter, he nevertheless gains dignity and stature. He is like his tutor, Sam Fathers, who was also a passive man of dignity, who passed on the virtues of the wilderness and his knowledge of patience, endurance, and compassion, as well as his knowledge of how to be worthy enough to kill noble and worthy game – and to love that which one kills.

Faulkner never meant for Ike to imitate the life of St. Paul or become an aggressive preacher or a crusading evangelist; instead, Isaac *himself decided* to emulate the Ancient Nazarene by becoming a simple carpenter and by living a simple life, independent of material things.

GO DOWN, MOSES

After reading the three magnificent stories concerning Ike's initiation and his relationship to the wilderness, many readers have been puzzled about Faulkner's choosing to end the book with a short story by the same name. By all standards, this story is something of an aftermath, when compared to the excellence of the preceding stories. Seemingly, on the surface, it is related to the other stories only by the presence of Mollie Beauchamp (Lucas' wife in "The Fire and the Hearth," where the name is spelled "Molly") and by the references to Roth Edmonds.

The simple story, however, *is* related to the other stories if we consider its emphasis upon *kinship* and *blood relationships.* Earlier, Ike was constantly concerned with his responsibilities to his ancestors, and here, in this story, the reverse is seen: old Mollie Beauchamp is not concerned with the crimes that her grandson *might have committed,* but rather, she is concerned that her grandson's body be returned to her for proper obsequies.

The story opens in the state penitentiary at Joliet, Illinois. A census taker finds out that a convicted murderer's real name is Samuel Worsham Beauchamp, and that his grandmother, Mollie Worsham Beauchamp, raised him. Note here that Lucas, the grandfather, is never mentioned, partly because, for Faulkner, the sense of the continuity of the family and the unity of the community is best exemplified through the women.

On the same day in Jefferson, Mississippi, Mollie, the grandmother, comes to the law offices of Gavin Stevens to hire him "to find my boy." After she leaves, Gavin is able to recall that Mollie's grandson is "Butch" Beauchamp, the bad son of a bad father who deserted his wife (Mollie's oldest daughter, who died in childbirth). "Butch" is now in the state penitentiary, accused of manslaughter.

Butch, we learn, was thrown off the McCaslin/Edmonds plantation long ago by Roth Edmonds for breaking into the commissary, and afterward, he spent the following year in and out of the county jail before he escaped, five years ago.

Thus, it is established early in the story that Butch Beauchamp is an unregenerate criminal – yet, for his grandmother who raised him, Butch is still her rightful grandson whose problems were all caused by Roth Edmonds when he threw Butch off the plantation.

In his first effort to find Mollie's grandson, Gavin goes to the county newspaper editor in search of information, and by a coincidence (perhaps too much of a coincidence to be believable), he sees a news release, where he learns that Samuel Worsham Beauchamp (a black man) of Jefferson, Mississippi, will be executed that night for the murder of a Chicago policeman. Returning to his office, Gavin finds a white woman, a Miss Worsham, who has come to help Mollie (a black woman), because Mollie and Mollie's brother, Hamp, and she were children together. Both Mollie and Hamp are descendants of slaves belonging to Miss Worsham's father, but both Mollie and Miss Worsham were raised together as sisters (despite the fact that one is black and the other is white), and in addition, Hamp and his wife still work for Miss Worsham.

Gavin is taken by surprise when Miss Worsham, ignoring Gavin's assertion about Butch's guilt and his evil nature, simply asserts that all that does not matter. All that matters is that Butch "must come home." Then she gives Gavin $25.00 in worn and crumpled bills and change, more money than she can afford, but not nearly enough to cover the expenses of "bringing Butch home."

Afterward, Gavin goes to the newspaper editor for a pledge, and then he goes from store to store, collecting money to bring back Mollie's grandson in a proper coffin, along with flowers, and a hearse to meet the train. Accordingly, Gavin involves a significant portion of the entire community of Jefferson in an effort to bring back a Negro murderer, merely to appease a grieving grandmother.

When Gavin visits Miss Worsham, he hears Mollie, later joined by her brother and sister-in-law, intoning lamentations for the dead grandson – "Done sold my Benjamin . . . Sold him in Egypt" – Gavin tries to convince her that it was *not* Roth's fault, but he realizes suddenly that *"she can't hear me."* In fact, Mollie is not even looking at Gavin. For Mollie, Roth Edmonds drove Butch off the plantation, out into the unknown world, and he is directly responsible for her grandson's death.

The final irony of the story, and one which Faulkner did not mean to be comic, is that Mollie wants her grandson's "death" to be reported in the newspaper – all about the funeral, and even though she can't read about it, she will be able to point to it. What her grandson had been in life no longer matters to Mollie. In death, however, she wants him to receive his full measure of respectful ritual burial – the casket, flowers, hearse, funeral procession, and his name in the newspaper. Then she will have fulfilled all of her obligations to her grandson.

It is interesting to note Mollie's *idée fixe*; she is convinced that Roth Edmonds sold her grandson into bondage. And she correlates her only grandson, Samuel/"Butch" with Benjamin of the Old Testament. Of course, however, it was Joseph of "the coat of many colors" who was actually sold into Egypt, and only years later, after Joseph had risen to power in the Egyptian government, and after his brothers came to buy grain, that Joseph "retained" his brother Benjamin. But, for Mollie's imperfect knowledge of the Bible, it is sufficient that *her* last-born was "sold" (cast out) out of his rightful land.

Some critics, such as Cleanth Brooks and Arthur Mizener, go to great lengths to show that the story is concerned with the plight of the intellectual (Gavin Stevens), trapped in the mores of a small Southern community, or else, they assert, the story shows the sense of the solidarity of the community when confronted with a problem. That is, Miss Worsham speaks of Mollie's grief as "our grief"; and the townspeople who have never even known "Butch" Beauchamp contribute toward having a Negro murderer's body returned to the community – "the merchants and clerks and barbers and professional men who had given Stevens the dollars and half dollars and quarters" – and eventually the entire community lines the streets to watch the hearse with the coffin and the flowers move around "the square, crossing it, circling the Confederate monument and the court house" before beginning its seventeen-mile journey to the McCaslin/Edmonds plantation. This image of the town square with the Confederate monument is the central image in almost all of Faulkner's novels; it represents the heart of his country – Yoknapatawpha.

In conclusion, most readers might expect Faulkner to end his book with the emphasis still on Isaac McCaslin, but as Faulkner often did (as in *Light in August,* for example), after the serious considerations of his hero's – in this case, Ike's – initiation, his awareness of his heritage, and his renunciation of his heritage, Faulkner chooses to end the novel with the emphasis upon a simple black woman's grief and on her discharging her obligations to her dead grandson, who is also a great-great-great-grandson of a rich, land-owning white man, old Lucius Quintus Carothers McCaslin.

SUGGESTED ESSAY QUESTIONS

1. Using specific details from "The Old People" and "The Bear," discuss the varying influences on Ike's maturation.

2. In "Was," discuss how *the hunt* (the dogs hunting the fox, the hunt for Tomey's Turl, and Miss Sophonsiba's hunt for a husband) is used as the basis for comedy.

3. "The Fire and the Hearth" was published as two separate stories. Discuss how Faulkner combines and unifies the two stories into one.

4. Discuss what values Ike learns from his association with Sam Fathers and from the wilderness.

5. What reasons could justify the inclusion of Part 4 in "The Bear"? Or justify excluding it.

6. How differently do Ike, Sam Fathers, Boon Hogganbeck, and Major de Spain view Old Ben?

7. Discuss how Part 5 of "The Bear" is related to Parts 1, 2, and 3.

8. Describe the difference between Ike McCaslin from his early life, his repudiation of his inheritance and, finally, as he is in "Delta Autumn."

SELECTED BIBLIOGRAPHY

BECK, WARREN. *Faulkner.* Madison: University of Wisconsin Press, 1976.

BLOTNER, JOSEPH. *Faulkner: A Biography.* New York: Random House, 1974.

BROOKS, CLEANTH. *William Faulkner: The Yoknapatawpha Country.* New Haven, Conn.: Yale University Press, 1963.

EARLY, JAMES. *The Making of Go Down, Moses.* Dallas, Tex.: Southern Methodist University Press, 1972.

GWYNN, FREDERICK L., and BLOTNER, JOSEPH L. *Faulkner in the University: Class Conferences at the University of Virginia, 1957–1958.* New York: Vintage Books, 1959.

HOFFMAN, FREDERICK J. *William Faulkner.* New Haven, Conn.: Twayne Publishers, 1966.

KLOTZ, MARVIN. "Procrustean Revision in Faulkner's *Go Down, Moses.*" *American Literature,* March 1965, pp. 1–16.

KUYK, DIRK, JR. *Threads Cable-strong.* Lewisburg, Pa.: Bucknell University Press, 1983.

MILLGATE, JANE. "Short Story into Novel: Faulkner's Reworking of 'Gold Is Not Always.'" *English Studies,* August 1964, pp. 310–17.

MILLGATE, MICHAEL. *The Achievement of William Faulkner.* New York: Random House, 1965.

REED, JOSEPH W., JR. *Faulkner's Narrative.* New Haven, Conn.: Yale University Press, 1973.

STEWART, DAVID H. "The Purpose of Faulkner's Ike." *Criticism* 3 (Fall 1961): 333–42.

102

SULTAN, STANLEY. "Call Me Ishmael: The Hagiography of Isaac McCaslin." *Texas Studies in Language and Literature,* Spring 1961, pp. 50–66.

TAYLOR, WALTER F., JR. "Let My People Go: The White Man's Heritage in *Go Down, Moses.*" *South Atlantic Quarterly,* Winter 1959, pp. 20–32.

TICK, STANLEY. "The Unity of *Go Down, Moses.*" *Twentieth Century Literature,* July 1962, pp. 67–73.

TRILLING, LIONEL. "The McCaslins of Mississippi." *The Nation,* May 30, 1942, pp. 632–33.

UTLEY, FRANCIS LEE, *et al.,* eds. *Bear, Man, and God: Seven Approaches to William Faulkner's "The Bear."* New York: Random House, 1964.

VICKERY, OLGA W. *The Novels of William Faulkner: A Critical Interpretation.* Baton Rouge: Louisiana State University Press, 1964.

WERTENBAKER, THOMAS J., JR. "Faulkner's Point of View and the Chronicle of Ike McCaslin." *College English,* December 1962, pp. 169–83.

NOTES

NOTES